JOAN OF ARC

*a
seven~
day
retreat*

Joan of Arc

GOD'S WARRIOR

BARBARA BECKWITH

ST. ANTHONY MESSENGER PRESS
Cincinnati, Ohio

Excerpts from *Joan of Arc: Her Story*, by Régine Pernoud and Marie-Véronique Clin, copyright ©1999, reprinted with permission of Palgrave Macmillan. "Prayer for Conscience and Courage in Times of Public Struggle," by Joan Chittister, O.S.B., copyright ©2007, reprinted with permission of Benetvision.

Cover and book design: Mark Sullivan

Cover image:
Rossetti, Dante Gabriel (1828–1882), Joan of Arc, 1864.
Tate Gallery, London, Great Britain
Photo credit: Tate Gallery, London / Art Resource, NY
Frame: www.istockphoto.com/Adam Korzekwa

Scripture passages have been taken from *New Revised Standard Version Bible*, copyright ©1989 by the Division of Christian Education of the National Council of the Churches of Christ in the U.S.A., and used by permission.
All rights reserved.

LIBRARY OF CONGRESS CATALOGING-IN-PUBLICATION DATA

Beckwith, Barbara, 1948-
Joan of Arc: God's warrior: a seven-day retreat / Barbara Beckwith.
p. cm.
Includes bibliographical references.
ISBN 978-0-86716-570-8 (pbk. : alk. paper) 1. Spiritual retreats—Catholic Church.
2. Joan, of Arc, Saint, 1412-1431. 3. Spirituality—Catholic Church. 4. Psychology, Religious. I. Title.

BX2376.5.B43 2007
269'.6—dc22

2007008747

ISBN 978-0-86716-570-8

Published by St. Anthony Messenger Press
28 W. Liberty St.
Cincinnati, OH 45202
www.AmericanCatholic.org

Printed in the United States of America.

Printed on acid-free paper.

07 08 09 10 11 5 4 3 2 1

To my uncle JAMES ROBERT NOLAN,

my godfather, who, as my guide through Paris and the Loire Valley

in France (among many other places throughout my life),

encouraged me to imagine Joan in the scenes before me and

suggested this book,

and my aunt MARY NOLAN READING,

my godmother, who challenged me to put the idea into reality,

saying, "Why not do it? What's stopping you?" Both of them

remembered that my middle name is Jean. I trust both are

enjoying being with Joan in heaven.

ACKNOWLEDGMENT

Since I have never studied French, I am indebted to the translating and editing skills of my colleague and bilingual friend Victoria E. Hébert of Quebec, Canada, and her family.

CONTENTS

GETTING TO KNOW OUR DIRECTOR

J OAN OF ARC CONTINUES TO FASCINATE US CENTURIES AFTER HER life and death. She is a bundle of contradictions: simple yet sublime, an illiterate peasant who held at bay the powerful and learned, a mystic whose earthy response to her visions was to inspire an army, a girl soldier who remained a virgin, a feminist long before the women's movement, a political prisoner who remained resolute yet wavered at critical times, a fiercely independent pawn of historical forces beyond her control, a glorious military hero who ended up a failure, betrayed by her friends and burned at the stake by her enemies.

Was she inspired? Was she mentally ill? Why did she do what she did? How did she find the courage? In the end, what did she accomplish? And what does a nineteen-year-old who lived from 1412 to 1431 have to teach us as our retreat director?

One of the words that keeps appearing in the written accounts of her is *mystery*. Her essence tantalizes, just beyond our grasp. She is open to many different interpretations, but actually her life is quite well-documented. Régine Pernoud, who was considered "the grande dame of French historical writing on the Middle Ages," says, "there is scarcely a chronicle or memoir from her time and place that does not mention her."[1] She left behind public and private letters that she dictated. She appears on the register of the Parlement of Paris. We have what amounts to transcripts (available on the Internet) of her two trials (one which condemned her when she was alive and one which nullified that first verdict twenty-five years after her death).

PLAYS, OPERAS, MOVIES ABOUND

There have been nearly five hundred years of efforts to make sense of Joan of Arc and discover what made her tick. The books, plays, operas and movies have been endless. As early as 1435, just four years after her death, *Le Mystère du siège d'Orléans*—a twenty thousand–verse play with more than a hundred speaking parts (written probably by Jacques Millet)—was performed.[2] (It was revised after the nullification trial.) William Shakespeare portrays her as "the English scourge"[3] in *Henry VI, Part I,* written between 1592 and 1594, but describes her as a sorceress, cursed by her father, thus justifying her fiery execution by the English.

Her story made it into several operas: Jacques Offenbach's in 1803, Giuseppe Verdi's in 1845, Charles Gounod's in 1873. Peter Ilich Tchaikovsky dedicated his first opera to Joan in 1879.[4]

In the twentieth century, stage depictions of Joan kept coming. George Bernard Shaw, an Irish Protestant, has his Saint Joan struggling against church and state, relying on her sense of mission and personal judgment. A French play, which underlined the "existentialist" character of Joan, was banned by the occupation authorities in 1942 because it might encourage resistance.

Jean Anouilh's *L'alouette (The Lark),* perhaps the most important post–World War II play about her, likens her to the classic Greek Antigone. Paul Claudel's text for the oratorio *Jeanne au bûche (Joan at the Stake)* emphasizes her lofty spirituality, which is complemented by the simplicity of Arthur Honegger's music.[5]

Cardinal Paul Poupard, president of the Pontifical Council for Culture, suggested in 2001 that the evolution of cinema is linked to treatment of Joan of Arc in film. "'Joan represents and perfectly incarnates the paradox' of a brief but extraordinarily intense life of events that were seemingly contradictory, he said. 'She is child and soldier, maid and patriot, devout and brutally condemned as a heretic....' Cardinal Poupard noted she is 'modern,' given her 'ambivalence, her multifaceted nature.'..."[6]

In movies, renowned actresses such as Ingrid Bergman and Jean Seberg put their own spins on the Joan role. As recently as 1999, Leelee Sobieski was luminous in Christian Duguay's *Joan of Arc,* which also starred Peter O'Toole and Olympia Dukakis. And in 2000 Milla Jovovich's Joan sported a bad haircut and fierce expressions in Luc Bresson's epic *The Messenger,* with John Malkovich, Faye Dunaway and Dustin Hoffman. Now American director-producer Ron Maxwell, who produced the films *Gettysburg* and *Gods and Generals* and the TV show *Christy,* has scouted locations for a movie tentatively titled *Joan of Arc: The Virgin Warrior,* which he promises will be an "epic."

On television the Arts and Entertainment channel even devoted one of its *Biography* shows to "Joan of Arc: Virgin Warrior," part of its *Legendary Women* series, which includes Mother Teresa, Jacqueline Kennedy Onassis and Anne Frank.

And CBS's award-winning but short-lived (2003–2006) TV series *Joan of Arcadia* raised for new generations the idea of taking direction directly from God. This Joan, played by actress Amber Tamblyn, thinks she's hearing the voice of God through various people in her life. Because the show ended so abruptly, no one will know if the heroine's instructions, like getting a job at a bookstore or befriending a special-needs child, were really coming from God or just hallucinations caused by Lyme disease. Plus, it's unknown if her paralyzed brother would ever walk (or dance, as one strange character predicted) or how she would have fared against the sinister young man (the devil perhaps?) introduced in the last few episodes, for he too claimed direct communication with God. The show ended in ambiguity, typical of artistic efforts to deal with Joan of Arc.

A QUESTION OF NAMES

The "mystery" of Joan begins with what to call her. "In my country [the region of Lorraine], people called me Jeannette, but they called me Jeanne when I came into France,"[7] she said at her condemnation trial. In the fifteenth century, most people went only by first names but sometimes added a place of origin or residence. She called herself "Jeanne la Pucelle" (Joan the Maid),[8] declaring chastity the sign of the purity of her mission. She had learned to sign her name as Jehannes and wrote it that way on several documents.

Pierre Cauchon, her chief judge, called her "Jehanne whom they call the Maid."[9] His colleagues at the University of Paris, who used Latin, referred to her as "*mulier quae Johannam se nominabat*" ("the woman who called herself Joan").[10]

"Of Arc" or "Darc" or "Tarc" first appears in her nullification trial when describing her brothers, Pierre and Jean, and mother, Isabelle. (Apostrophes came into use later to connote local origin or membership in the nobility.) In French, "arc" refers to a bow. A 1612 account of her life says that "the very arms of the parents and other descendants of the aforesaid Jacques Darc [her father]...carried a bow with three arrows...."[11]

In general today, English speakers refer to her as "Joan" and French speakers call her "Jeanne." Although it was the language of her enemy, English is my native tongue, so I have chosen to refer to the maid as Joan in this book. I hope she accepts my apologies for this.

Even though her second trial cleared Joan of heresy, it was not until 1909 that she was beatified. The fact that it took over 450 years to have the church recognize her as a holy person to be emulated shows the ambiguities in her life (and the embarrassment she was to the church because it had been an ecclesiastical trial that had condemned her). But then her canonization proceeded with remarkable speed. During the nineteenth century she had become the romantic soul of France, its national heroine. Many French soldiers during World War I had a particular devotion to her, which may have sped up the canonization process, for she was declared a saint in 1920.

A PRODUCT OF WAR

World War I was very much like the Hundred Years' War of Joan's time. The Hundred Years' War refers to "a series of destructive wars between France and England" between 1337 and 1453.[12] It was a "total war," which involved the whole population. Its aims were not clear. A large part of it took place on French soil. Both armies got mired down; the battles claimed many lives; thousands were maimed, and the war seemed interminable.

The French and English monarchies were incredibly entwined during the Hundred Years' War. Two of the feudal principalities (Aquitaine and Burgundy), which should have been subject to the king of France, were now wealthier and more powerful than the king. The duke of Aquitaine was also king of England (the result of Eleanor of Aquitaine's marriage to Henry II of England in 1152—remember the movie *The Lion in Winter*?). The duke of Burgundy was count of Flanders and of some neighboring states in the Low

Countries and Rhineland, and he was becoming richer because of the capitalism beginning to emerge from the feudalism there.

A succession crisis triggered the war. In 1329, the Capetian line of kings, which had provided stability to France since 996, ended when Charles IV died without surviving sons. Charles was the last of three sons of Philip IV. Two of his nephews claimed the crown of France: Philip of Valois, who claimed descent from the Capetian line, and Edward III of England, whose mother was a daughter of Philip IV. Inheritance law of the time would have said that Edward had the greater claim, but a French court ruled otherwise because the inheritance in question was the kingdom of France. The court decided in favor of the Valois line, not the Plantagenet's claim. In 1337 Edward challenged Philip, by then King Philip VI, to "a trial by combat."[13]

Four phases marked the Hundred Years' War.[14] In the first phase (1337–1360), the Plantagenets were triumphant, with victories at sea (Sluis) and on land (Crecy in 1346 and Poitiers in 1356). The Valois king, John II, was captured, with the Treaty of Brétigny assigning more northern territories to Edward and setting John's ransom at a high sum calculated to bankrupt the French treasury.

In the second phase (1360–1413), Charles V (the Wise) of France chipped away at many of the concessions of the Treaty of Brétigny, reclaimed territory that had been lost and reestablished order after peasant uprisings had been brutally put down by the nobility. The French success was aided by a crisis within the English monarchy. The eldest son of Edward III had died before his father; Richard II, who acceded to the English throne, was deposed by his cousin, Henry of Lancaster, thereafter known as Henry IV.

There were strains on the French side as well. At Charles the Wise's death, a rivalry between two of his supporters, Duke John the

Fearless of Burgundy and his first cousin, Duke Louis of Orléans, ended in the assassination of Louis. The royalist Valois faction seeking revenge was led by Count Bernard VII of Armagnac, which sits on the border of the Plantagenet Aquitaine and loyalist France in the southern part of the kingdom. (The Valois faction came to be known as Armagnacs.) The French king Charles VI eventually went mad, earning the sobriquet Charles the Mad.

The third phase (1413–1428) lasted from the succession of Henry V, the second Lancastrian king, to the siege of Orléans. In between was the English victory at Agincourt (1415), prompting the Treaty of Troyes, which awarded Charles VI's daughter Catherine in marriage to Henry and declared that their future son (Henry VI) would be king of both France and England. But this provision disinherited Charles, the dauphin, fifth son of Charles the Mad but the only son left alive in 1422 when Henry V of England died. The dauphin took refuge in Bourges, slightly south of Paris and the geographical center of France, and engaged in bumbling efforts to regain control.

Upon Henry's death, his brother, the Duke of Bedford, vigorously prosecuted the war, aided by an alliance with Duke Philip the Good of Burgundy. In 1428 Philip laid siege to Orléans to clear the way for an all-out attack on the dauphin. An English victory seemed assured.

It is at this point that Joan appeared on the scene, ushering in the fourth and final phase of the war (1429–1453). She inspired the deliverance of Orléans and propelled the dauphin to Reims for his anointing and coronation. The Anglo-Burgundian alliance engineered Joan's death at Rouen in 1431 but could not undo the French military recovery she initiated. Four years later the Treaty of Arras ended the Armagnac-Burgundian feud. In 1453 the English were nearly completely expelled from French soil.

Though mercifully not as long, the Vietnam War of the 1960s and '70s and the current Afghanistan and Iraq wars should give Americans some sympathy for what the French of the fourteenth and fifteenth centuries went through. But none of these was conducted on American soil. To get some sense of the devastating, demoralizing effect of this French war, think of the American Civil War.

A CHURCH RECOVERING FROM SCHISM

Joan was also a victim of the Great Schism in the church, when two popes claimed control, one in Rome, one in Avignon, a papal city on the Rhône River directly across from southern France. In addition, from 1409 to 1415 there was even a third claimant!

Earlier, Pope Boniface VIII (pope from 1294 to 1303) had died escaping from French troops under King Philip IV of France, who had come into Italy to arrest him.[15] His successor was the archbishop of Bordeaux in France, who took the name of Clement V and endorsed Philip's major religious policies, like the destruction of the Knights Templar. He moved the permanent residence of the pope from Rome to Avignon. There was so much outrage throughout Europe about this move that eventually (in 1376) the papacy returned to Rome, to general approval, even in France.

Two years later, a disputed election produced two popes, each claiming the throne of Peter. One pope stayed in Rome; the other went to Avignon. A church council at Pisa in 1409, struggling to rectify the issue, only succeeded in bringing forth a third pope. In 1415, the papal situation was resolved when a general council was finally recognized as superior to the office of pope. The restored papacy in Rome was headed by a native Roman, Martin V (1417– 1431), but worked to overturn the reform that had put him in place.

During the schism, the English king and parliament had supported the Roman pope, because the French kings supported the one in Avignon. The Scots, trying to carve out a stance independent of the English, supported the Avignon claimant.

Both popes excommunicated their rivals and the supporters of their rivals, denying them the sacraments.

The hope for ending this scandal and reforming the church lay in a commitment to the institution of the general council.[16] Thousands of clerics and laymen from every part of Christendom met in Constance, a city on the upper Rhine between 1414 and 1417. A second council met in nearby Basel between 1431 and 1437. The University of Paris faculty favored conciliar reform and supported the Plantagenet claim to the French crown. They hoped a dual monarch of both France and England would have his hands so full that he would rely more on the parliamentary institutions of both countries. It was their hope for more democratic government that spawned their furious opposition to Joan, who they saw as representing a return to absolutism, royal and papal.[17]

A LIFE CUT SHORT, TOLD BRIEFLY

The youngest of five children, Joan was born on January 6, 1431, in Domrémy-Greux, which is along the winding Meuse River, to the east and slightly south of Paris. Her father, Jacques, was a farmer, fairly well-to-do for a peasant. In 1423, Jacques was chosen doyen for the village, which meant he commanded the day and night watches, supervised the weights and measures, collected taxes and rents, and promulgated the decrees of the village council.[18]

Joan was only twelve when she experienced the first of her visions, which she described as a voice or voices accompanied by blazing light. Later, she came to identify the voices as those of Saint Michael the Archangel, Saint Catherine and Saint Margaret. She claimed they revealed to her that she had a mission to save France by aiding the dauphin.

One of her prophecies came true when the French were defeated at the Battle of Herrings (related to a supply train of herrings for the besieged city of Orléans) in 1429. This gained her the support of Robert de Baudricourt, the French commander at Vaucouleurs, who sent her on to the dauphin, as she requested. The dissolute young man was at the palace at Chinon, along the Loire River. According to legend, he disguised himself to test if Joan could recognize him, which she did. (Today this scene is staged with life-sized mannequins at Chinon.) He became convinced of her mission and put her in charge of an expedition to relieve the besieged Orléans, after having her examined by theologians at Poitiers to ensure she was not in heresy.

At Orléans she led her forces to victory. (Copies of the banners carried by her forces are still in the cathedral there.) This was followed with a victory over the British at Troyes, where she captured the city. Finally, on July 17, 1429, she was next to Charles, when he was crowned King Charles VII at Reims.

Joan failed in an attempt to capture Paris in August 1428, and was captured in May 1429 near Compiègne, held in a tower in Beaurevoir for months, and sold to the British by John of Luxemburg on November 21 of that year. She was then moved to Rouen.

She was charged with "lack of submission to the Church Militant,"[19] and with the wearing of men's clothes. Her accusers were convinced that her visions had their source in the devil, and that she practiced witchcraft. The judge, Bishop Pierre Cauchon of Beauvais, theologians with whom he had taught at the University of Paris, assessors and others tried many ways to trip her up, but she withstood four months of their constant questioning. Under intense political pressure from the British and because she went back to wearing men's clothes (perhaps due to a rape attempt in prison), Cauchon condemned her to death. In the end, wearing men's clothes was the only charge that held up, which was considered a deliberate relapse into error, a visible sign of her refusal to submit to the church.

On May 30, 1431, Joan was led from prison to the Old Marketplace in Rouen and burned at the stake there. She asked to have a cross and died crying out the name of Jesus. Her ashes were collected and scattered in the Seine River, "so that no relics could be claimed later."[20]

It wasn't until 1920 that she was canonized a saint in the Catholic church.

MY INTEREST IN JOAN

Because my middle name is Jean, I have always had an interest in Joan of Arc. She was much more exciting to me than Saint Barbara, a virgin and martyr from fourth-century Rome. In fifth grade, when we had to dress as our patron saint for Halloween (a Catholic school's attempt to Christianize a pagan celebration), I chose to come as Joan of Arc in battle garb, silver metallic material being more interesting to me than a draped sheet to simulate a Roman toga.

On May 16, 1966, just before I entered Marquette University that fall to study journalism (with minors in history and theology), the St. Joan of Arc Chapel on the campus in Milwaukee, Wisconsin, was dedicated. The simple Gothic chapel, originally known as the Chappelle de St. Martin de Sayssuel, had stood in the little French village of Chasse, about twelve miles south of Lyon and six miles north of Vienne, in the Rhône River Valley. Tradition has it that Joan prayed in this chapel before leading troops into battle in 1429.

One stone in the chapel is always colder than its neighbors. It is here, legend has it, that Joan stood and prayed before a statue of Our Lady. Then she kissed that stone. I can personally attest to its extraordinary coolness. I often used to attend the intimate Masses in the chapel, which holds only about one hundred people. I would stop in for quick visits to pray before tests (especially calculus), before presentations at theology seminars, before news stories were due with only three hours remaining until the deadline. I figured that the illiterate Joan would help her spiritual "daughter" to a good education. Usually, she came through; when she didn't, it was because I had not done my part.

During protests over the Vietnam War in the late '60s, we students often held rallies on this spot. In 1969, we protesters "took over" the chapel to get the university administration's attention— and we did. It was our belief that the war being waged in Vietnam did not qualify as a "just war," as Joan's had been. The Joan of Arc chapel seemed a fitting place to preach revolution.

In my travels since college I have been to France many times, traveling through nearly all the places associated with the Joan story, except for her birthplace, Domrémy. I have been to Chinon, where Joan recognized the dauphin and was given his approval to gather an army and pursue his claim to the throne of France. I've been to Notre Dame Cathedral in Paris where there are statues of her, inside and outside, but also where she was defeated. I've picnicked along the Loire River where she gathered her troops and marched them to Orléans. I've been to the cathedral of that city which still celebrates her efforts to end its many-year siege and keep it out of English hands. Another year I was in Rouen on her feast day of May 30 and joined a procession that marks her journey to her execution.

She is my soul sister as a feminist and an independent woman who marched to her own drummer.

Notes

1. Régine Pernoud and Marie-Véronique Clin, *Joan of Arc: Her Story*, Jeremy duQuesnay Adams, trans., Bonnie Wheeler, ed. (New York: St. Martin's Griffin, 1998) (Originally published as *Jeanne d'Arc*, Régine Pernoud and M.-V. Clin [Paris: Librairie Arthème Fayard, 1986]), p. xii.
2. Pernoud and Clin, p. 237.
3. William Shakespeare, *Henry VI, Part I*, Act I, Scene II.
4. Pernoud and Clin, p. 238.
5. Pernoud and Clin, p. 240.
6. Zenit News Service, "Joan of Arc: Pivotal Throughout History of Cinema," Rome, December 9, 2001. http://www.zenit.org/english/visualizza.phtml?sid=13832.
7. Pernoud and Clin, p. 220.
8. Pernoud and Clin, p. 220.
9. Pernoud and Clin, p. 220.
10. Pernoud and Clin, p. 220.
11. Pernoud and Clin, p. 220.
12. Pernoud and Clin, p. 1.
13. Pernoud and Clin, p. 2.
14. Pernoud and Clin, p. 2.
15. Pernoud and Clin, p. 4.
16. Pernoud and Clin, p. 5.
17. Pernoud and Clin, p. 6.
18. Pernoud and Clin, p. 221.
19. Pernoud and Clin, p. 126.
20. Pernoud and Clin, p. 137.

DAY ONE

LISTENING

TO

MYSTICAL

VOICES

"When we reflect that her century was the brutalest, the wickedest, the rottenest in history since the darkest ages, we are lost in wonder at the miracle of such a product from such a soil. The contrast between her and her century is the contrast between day and night. She was truthful when lying was the common speech of men; she was honest when honesty was become a lost virtue; she was a keeper of promises when the keeping of a promise was expected of no one;...she was steadfast when stability was unknown, and honorable in an age which had forgotten what honor was; she was a rock of convictions in a time when men believed nothing and scoffed at all things; she was unfailingly true in an age that was false to the core....

"She was perhaps the only entirely unselfish person whose name has a place in profane history."

—Mark Twain[1]

INTRODUCING OUR RETREAT THEME

Mark Twain was quite enamored of Joan of Arc and spent twelve years researching his book about her. He starts out trying to distance her from her age—yet ends up distancing her from us by such effusive praise.

Actually, what came out in the nullification trial, when the court took the time to gather witnesses from her family, village and comrades-in-arms, was that she was very ordinary, "except for her notable piety."[2] Her *willingness* was particularly remembered:

> She went often and *willingly* to church and holy places.... She *willingly* took care of the animals of her father's house.... She confessed herself *willingly*.... She worked *willingly* and took care of many responsibilities, spun, did housework, went to help with harvests, and when it was time, sometimes, she watched over the animals while spinning.[3]

What started to set Joan apart was the peculiar experience she had of hearing voices, starting in adolescence—some biographies say as early as age twelve. Hearing voices no one else heard confused her, but in the end she decided to act on what they told her. She didn't always understand the things they were saying or why they were saying them to her. She may have gotten some things wrong, but she kept trying to hear them and discern what God wanted of her.

What began in mystical experience turned into one year of military victories and one year as a political prisoner—her entire adult life.

In the end, she died a martyr's death, wanting to keep her eyes focused on a cross, calling out the name of Jesus. She persevered in faith, steadfast unto death. She was like the Old Testament prophets that the author of the Letter to the Hebrews describes: They "through faith conquered kingdoms, administered justice, obtained promises, shut the mouths of lions...won strength out of weakness, became mighty in war, put foreign armies to flight" and ended up tortured, mocked, in chains and imprisoned and finally killed (11:33, 35–37).

But because of their inspiring faith and because they now surround us like "so great a cloud of witnesses," great spirits like Joan encourage us to "lay aside every weight and the sin that clings so closely, and let us run with perseverance the race that is before us, looking to Jesus..." (12:1–2).

Opening Prayer

Dear God,
our friend Joan of Arc
was once a child to whom
you sent your angels and saints.
Help us to listen
to all the angels and saints you send us,
especially those disguised as
our fellow companions in faith.
Amen.

Retreat Session One

"My Voices *did* come from God and everything I have done was by God's order."

—Joan of Arc[4]

It all began for Joan in 1424 with hearing voices.

One summer day in her father's garden, she heard a mysterious voice, which was accompanied by a bright light. "At first I was very much frightened," she said later. "The voice came toward the hour of noon. I had fasted the preceding day. I heard the voice on my right hand, in the direction of the church. I seldom hear it without seeing a light. The light always appears on the side from which I hear the voice."[5]

Joan came to identify this voice as belonging to Saint Michael the Archangel, the one who drove Lucifer out of heaven. The warrior angel, he is usually depicted with a flaming sword. *Michael* (Mi-ka-'El) means "Who is like to God?" in Hebrew. (The other archangels have similar names, *Gabriel* means "strength of God" and *Raphael*, "God heals.") Michael is mentioned three times in the Old Testament, particularly in the book of Daniel (10:13–21; 12:1), where he is the defender of the Israelites and the head of a heavenly army that defends the weak and oppressed.

In the New Testament book of Revelation, Michael battles the dragon who tried to snatch the child born of the "woman clothed with the sun, with the moon under her feet, and on her head a crown of twelve stars" (12:1). Then

> ...war broke out in heaven; Michael and his angels fought against the dragon. The dragon and his angels fought back, but they were defeated, and there was no longer any place for them in heaven. The great dragon was thrown down, that ancient serpent who is called the Devil and Satan, the deceiver of the whole world—he was thrown down to the earth, and his angels were thrown down with him. (12:7–9)

Because of Saint Michael, the devil knows his time on earth is short (see 12:12).

For this reason, a booklet about the Saint Michael Shrine on the Gargano in Italy says, "Christians consider the Archangel Saint Michael as the most powerful defender of God's people."[6]

Joan later came to identify the other saints she heard as Saint Catherine (most likely Saint Catherine of Alexandria, patron of young girls and of a nearby parish at Maxy-sur-Meuse) and Saint Margaret (most likely Saint Margaret of Antioch, whose statue is still in Joan's home parish church at Domrémy).[7] (Catherine and Margaret were eliminated from the church's calendar in 1969 for three reasons: (1) So little information exists about them; (2) only some 125 saints among the thousands canonized have feast days;

and (3) the church was trying to make its calendar more global by rotating off some European and older saints. That same reform axed Saints Christopher and Barbara.)

The Archangel Michael's, however, remains solidly as a September feast, although Michaelmas (September 29) now includes the other archangels. Whenever people see themselves as facing evil and needing to battle against injustice, Michael has been invoked. After Masses in the 1950s, in particular, the church called upon Saint Michael to help defeat Communism.[8] The same was probably true in the fifteenth century as the French found themselves in a brutal occupation by the English where pillage, rape and killing of civilians were common.

It was, in fact, Saint Michael who appeared to Joan first. "It was St. Michael whom I saw before my eyes, and he was not alone but was well accompanied by angels of heaven.... I saw them with the eyes of my body as well as I see you," she told one of her interrogators, Jean Beaupère, a canon of Rouen. She added, "and when they left me I wept and wished that they would have taken me with them."[9]

Joan more often heard these saints than saw them. Even though she claims to have seen them sometimes, she could not describe their appearance. In fact, she was amused when asked if they had hair. When asked if Saint Margaret spoke English, she responded: "How should she speak English, since she is not of the English party?"[10] (By that time the languages of France and England were distinct from each other.[11]) Another time she told Friar Pierre Sequin, described as a specialist in holy Scripture, that her voices spoke better than he did, a reference to the fact that Sequin had a thick accent as he came from Limoges.[12]

"Filled with both fear and elation she told no one of this supernatural experience, not her village priest to whom she often confessed, not even her parents."[13] It came out later, especially at her trial. The whole charge of witchcraft turned on whether these voices were heaven-sent or from the devil, whether she summoned demons to help her. The English were at a loss to explain otherwise how she could have beaten them.

MYSTICAL EXPERIENCE

"Hearing voices no one else can hear isn't a good sign, even in the wizarding world," Ron Weasley warns Harry in *Harry Potter and the Chamber of Secrets*. (In the movie it's Hermione Grainger who stops on the central staircase of Hogwarts School of Witchcraft and Wizardry to express this truism, with the moving portraits behind her concurring.)[14] Hearing voices can be a sign of mental illness— or the form mystical experience takes. Mystical experience is communication with God.

The word *mystic* comes from the Greek *mystikos* or *mystos*, which means "mysteries." "Broadly speaking, all Christians are mystics. We believe that by faith we are initiated into the mysteries of Christ's death and resurrection."[15] In fact, the church today has tried to reincorporate that sense of the mysteries by bringing back the mystagogia for the newly baptized in the period after Easter, a time to bring them more deeply into the heart of the Christian teachings, its "mysteries."

Usually being a mystic is a solitary experience. Mystics are set apart by direct knowledge of God or spiritual truth. Mystics are in touch with the supernatural, without the aid of the senses or logic.

C.G. Jung's study of human nature, which developed into the personality types of the Myers-Briggs indicator, suggests that people are innately either sensates (who depend more on the information they get from their senses) or intuitive (who trust more their own instincts and mental constructs). But mystics ratchet intuition up a notch. They claim direct knowledge of God, spiritual truth or ultimate reality—and have no idea how to explain what they know. They just *know*.

MENTAL ILLNESS?

Because of the unexplainable nature of their insights, some mystics can seem deluded or mentally ill. New research has discovered that religious experience is processed in a particular part of the brain.[16] Surprising as it seems, there is a biological basis for religious experience. But that part of the brain is dangerously close to parts that do control sanity, which is why many mentally ill people first "get religion."

Saint Paul, describing his own religious experience, says, "For if we are beside ourselves [sometimes *insane* is used for the Greek *exestemen*], it is for God; if we are in our right mind, it is for you" (2 Corinthians 5:13). He goes on to talk about a man he knew who "heard things that are not to be told, that no mortal is permitted to repeat" and boasts of going "on to visions and revelations of the Lord" (2 Corinthians 12:4, 1).

Did Joan suffer from a mental illness? Were her voices the result of that illness? Many mental illnesses begin in adolescence, about the age Joan started hearing her voices.

Historian Karen Armstrong is known today for her scholarly books like *A History of God: The 4,000-Year Quest of Judaism, Christianity and Islam* and *Holy War: The Crusades and Their Impact on Today's World*. But in the early 1970s as a struggling graduate student in England, she suffered from hallucinations. It turned out that she suffered from temporal lobe epilepsy. The doctor who finally diagnosed her commented, "[I]t's interesting that you were once a nun. People with temporal lobe epilepsy are often religious!"[17] For Joan, however, there is little evidence that she had physical seizures, "fits" or "staring spells" or "zoned out" for periods of time. If so, nobody seems to have noticed.

Another illness, schizophrenia, can be similarly pinpointed to a nearby part of the brain. Schizophrenics often have visual, auditory and other sensory hallucinations. Joan testified that she had not only seen and heard Saint Catherine and Saint Margaret but also had embraced them, kissed their feet and noted that they smelled good. Schizophrenics may believe they are powerful or on a mission, or they may fixate on certain ideas. Certainly, Joan claimed she was on a mission from God and was preoccupied with trying to give the French back a French king. Nonetheless, Joan could concentrate well on details such as military strategy. She was very self-possessed, aware of her identity and role. She showed none of the bizarre behavior and incomprehensible speech that often accompanies schizophrenia.[18]

It also doesn't seem that she suffered from bipolar disorder (which used to be called manic depression); she wasn't moody, and her ability to think was not impaired.

Were Joan's voices real or not? This will be debated for a long time to come. Teenagers, especially girls, are often intensely emotional—even when they aren't mentally ill—and *intense* definitely describes Joan. Her visions were accompanied by a flurry of emotions: special and important, on the one hand, and isolated and depressed, on the other. Above all, she was confused and struggling to make sense of it all—for about a quarter of her short life—before taking action. What I know is that she believed her voices were real. Since their "fruits," if you will, changed the course of history and freed an oppressed people, I, for one, will stick with the judgment that Joan heard something heaven-sent and was sane enough to figure out how to turn her visions into reality.

HARNESSING MYSTICAL EXPERIENCES

I usually have my feet anchored on the ground, but I've had two mystical experiences, both involving family members who had just died. My seventy-eight-year-old grandmother, who suffered from breast cancer that had turned into bone cancer, had been in a coma for three weeks. We all knew she was going to die, but I, living three hundred miles away, knew the exact moment she went home to God. I telephoned my mother; she didn't know that Nana had died yet, but then quickly confirmed it. But I had known—I had felt Nan's quick kiss as she left us.

More than twenty years later, my aunt Mary died of lung cancer diagnosed only three days earlier, and her husband, six children, their spouses and I were struggling to plan her funeral liturgy. After three hours of debating, we selected the readings and some hymns, but couldn't move to the intercessions. We were just going to let the celebrant worry about that. But that night, I heard Mary call me out of a deep sleep. I went to the door of the B&B guest room where I was staying, and saw no one there. But the voice I had heard had definitely been hers—she often used to wake me and I knew it well. She said nothing but my name, but I instantly knew that what she wanted was for me to write the intercessions for the Mass, using my talent as a writer to help pull her grieving family together. I felt inspired in the writing the next morning, and the intercessions did help. Her voice, like my grandmother's presence, had been gentle— like their spirits.

Both of my experiences involved members of my family, but I believe firmly in the communion of saints. Why wouldn't Saint

Michael, Saint Catherine and Saint Margaret help us if they could?

Can mystical experiences be useful? Young people always struggle to discern a career path and make some basic life choices. In midlife we reevaluate those choices and may change direction. As we age, our experiences of God need to be examined, and we should make room in our hearts for a bigger God. Joan teaches us not to ignore the deepest yearnings of our hearts, the things we know and desire but maybe cannot express. Those mystical insights that we all have need to be acknowledged and harnessed to make better prudential judgments.

FOR REFLECTION

1. When have you experienced God? Do you find God most often in prayer, at Mass or a religious service, at sunrise or sunset, while staring at the ocean or the sky, confronted with a lovely landscape or city vista, while looking through a telescope or microscope, when you look at religious art? Where else?

2. Have you had any answers in prayer that you cannot understand, that you still don't understand perhaps years later? Have you ever had a mystical experience, an experience involving someone who has died, a foreknowledge of something that will happen? How did you react?

3. Which saints would you most want to hear from?

4. Would Saint Michael be a good patron for these times when terrorism means everyone is at risk?

5. Is God trying to tell you something, but you have put up barriers to tune out the message?

CLOSING PRAYER

"God,
if today I hear your voice,
harden not my heart."[19]
Open my eyes
and my heart
to see you and hear you.
May I really listen to all you are telling me today.
Let us see the many ways
you are working in our world,
in my world.
Let me feel your constant presence
and the warmth of your love.
Amen.

Notes

1. Mark Twain, *Joan of Arc* (San Francisco: Ignatius, 1989), pp. 19–20.
2. Pernoud and Clin, p. 161.
3. Pernoud and Clin, p. 162.
4. http://www.stjoan-center.com/quotable.
5. Bert Ghezzi, *Mystics and Miracles: True Stories of Lives Touched by God* (Chicago: Loyola, 2002), p, 150.
6. P. Jan Bogacki, CSMA, Christine Fesq, trans. *Saint Michael Shrine on the Gargano* (second Edition "Michael," 2001), p. 46.
7. Pernoud and Clin, p. 113.
8. The prayer is as follows: "Saint Michael the Archangel, defend us in the day of battle; be our safeguard against the wickedness and snares of the devil. May God rebuke him, we humbly pray, and do you, O prince of the heavenly host, by the power of God, cast into hell Satan and all the other evil spirits who prowl through the world, seeking the ruin of souls. Amen." Available in "Prayer to Saint Michael," *Catholic Prayers for Every Day and All Day*, Leonard Foley, O.F.M., and Patti Normile, eds. (Cincinnati, Ohio: St. Anthony Messenger Press, 2004), p. 95.
9. Pernoud and Clin, p. 113.
10. Pernoud and Clin, p. 115.
11. Pernoud and Clin, p. 223.
12. Pernoud and Clin, p. 29.
13. Polly Schoyer Brooks, *Beyond the Myth: The Story of Joan of Arc* (Boston: Houghton Mifflin, 1990), p. 24.
14. J.K. Rowling, *Harry Potter and the Chamber of Secrets* (New York: Scholastic, 1999), p. 145.
15. Ghezzi, p. xi.
16. Rita Carter, *Mapping the Brain* (Berkeley, Calif.: University of California Press, 1999).
17. Karen Armstrong, *The Spiral Staircase: My Climb Out of Darkness* (New York: Anchor, 2005), p. 182.
18. Judy Grundy, "Joan of Arc Considered." Available at www.stjoan-center.com/topics/jgrundy.html.
19. Psalm 95:7–8, used as the daily invitatory for *The Liturgy of the Hours*, International Commission on English in the Liturgy, trans. (New York: Catholic Book Publishing, 1975).

DAY TWO

STEPPING

OUT

IN

FAITH

"...Joan of Arc, a mere child in years, ignorant, unlettered, a poor village girl unknown and without influence, found a great nation lying in chains, helpless and hopeless under an alien domination, its treasury bankrupt, its soldiers disheartened and dispersed, all spirit torpid, all courage dead in the hearts of the people through long years of foreign and domestic outrage and oppression, their King cowed, resigned to its fate, and preparing to fly the country; and she laid her hand upon this nation, this corpse, and it rose and followed her. She led it from victory to victory, she turned back the tide of the Hundred Years' War, she fatally crippled the English power, and died with the earned title of DELIVERER OF FRANCE, which she bears to this day."

—Mark Twain[1]

COMING TOGETHER IN THE SPIRIT

What seems to have impressed Mark Twain the most was the fact that, at the age of seventeen, Joan took command of an army. She remains the youngest "general" in history—of either sex. Samuel Clemens (as he was born) was a Union Army deserter in the Civil War. Admitting Joan was "the *Riddle* of the Ages,"[2] Twain was a Protestant who could see the value of action.

Unlike many visionaries who are overwhelmed by their visions, Joan acted on hers. She stepped out in faith and acted on what her voices told her to do. Persevering in faith means that we do not allow ourselves to be paralyzed into inaction because we don't understand everything or are unable to predict the consequences of our actions. Rather than complaining about the English occupation of her land, she did something. Mind you, most people who hear voices should not go grab a gun, but Joan's call to arms was for the sake of France.

Trying to put Joan into perspective, Siobhan Nash-Marshall suggests:

> Joan was a *quester*: an individual who had a powerful sense of purpose, an extraordinary mission. One characteristic common to all questers, is that they become their quests, in some sense. Socrates was the gadfly of Athens, Aristotle her philosopher, St. Francis was God's troubadour, St. Thomas his scientist. Questers live for their quests and see no life outside of their quests. Their spectacular focus is what gives them their strength.[3]

It also leads them to challenge the status quo and the social mores of the times. "Joan could hardly have changed the course of history if she had let herself be bothered by the unwritten medieval rule that held that noblemen alone could be *chefs de guerre*. Nor could she have led and lived with an army if she had attempted to accommodate social mores."[4]

OPENING PRAYER
    God,
    you called Joan
    to step out in faith
    and work to secure justice
    for her people.

What do you ask of me—
here?
now?
Amen.

RETREAT SESSION TWO
"Help yourself and God will help you."

—Joan of Arc[5]

This characteristic saying of Joan's is the French equivalent of "God helps those who help themselves."

Joan's family's experiences as war refugees sharpened Joan's political resolve. On the other side of the Meuse River from Domrémy was the English-controlled Lorraine. In June 1428, when Joan was sixteen, the English were preparing to "lay waste" to the neighborhood of Vaucouleurs, which includes Domrémy. So her family "carrying their possessions, and driving their livestock, fled south to the fortified town of Neufchâteau."[6]

There, the family stayed with an innkeeper, Madame la Rousse. Later, at Joan's first trial, it was charged that the inn was a brothel and Joan a prostitute there, but these accusations were proved false. It was from an incident at Neufchâteau that Joan was summoned into a court in Toul and accused of having broken a promise to marry. The marriage had probably been arranged by her parents, as was the custom. But Joan won the case, proving that she had never given any pledge to marry. This incident shows "bold independence, if not defiance" on Joan's part.[7]

Upon the family's return to Domrémy, they found the village destroyed. Even the church had been burned. Now came the news that the strategic city of Orléans was under siege and another key city, the nearby Vaucouleurs, was about to be surrendered by the governor, Robert de Baudricourt.

For Joan, it was time to do what her voices had been telling her. Under the ruse of helping her cousin who had just had a baby and lived in a village outside Vaucouleurs, Joan left home. She was in the care of her cousin's husband, Durand Laxart. (She called Laxart "uncle," since he was fifteen years older than she.) She begged Laxart to introduce her to the governor, so that she could enlist his help in getting to the dauphin. At first, Baudricourt told Laxart, "Take her home and tell her father to box her ears."[8]

While waiting around hoping Baudricourt would change his mind, Joan made friends with one of Baudricourt's young knights, Jean Metz (also known as Jean Neuillonpont, since that was his home village on the Othain River). Metz pledged his allegiance to her.

News of this strange, pious girl was spreading. The duke of Lorraine asked to see her, although he was pro-Burgundian. He had hoped that this young girl could heal him. She told him she knew nothing about healing but dared to add that he would do well to give up his mistress. Then she had the nerve to ask for his help to get to Chinon, and he gave her some gold pieces and a black horse.

After she returned to Vaucouleurs, she surprised Baudricourt by telling him that the French had been defeated by the English in a battle near Orléans. (Her "voices" may have told her, but it was not generally known yet.) When Baudricourt found out her news was true, he decided to support her, after insisting that she be exorcised of demons. He gave Joan another horse and a small retinue, and allowed Metz to accompany her on the three-hundred-fifty-mile trip to Chinon.

Although the dauphin had already agreed to see her, he kept her waiting for an audience. Finally summoned to the palace hall, Joan found some three hundred knights surrounding him. Somehow, Joan made straight for the dauphin. Remember that this was before newspapers or television to give her any visual clues, and she had never seen him before. (Some legends say he switched clothes with one of his courtiers—the better to confuse and test her. But she knew him immediately.) She told Charles that she would last a little longer than a year, and there was much work to be done in that short time.[9]

Charles took Joan with him and his court as they moved to Poitiers, and she endured three weeks of questioning by his theological advisers under the leadership of the archbishop of Reims. One told her, "You have said that a voice told you that God wishes to deliver the people of France from their present calamity. If He wants to deliver them, it is not necessary to send soldiers." Joan responded, "In the name of God, the soldiers will fight and God will deliver them."[10] She was also subjected to a test of virginity, by female inspectors, and passed that, too.

Then it was off to war.

WORLD'S FIRST PROTESTANT?

"What you hear in the dark / you must speak in the light. / You are salt for the earth; / you are light for the world," the antiphon for Dan Schutte's song reminds us.[11] Christians must use their insights to build the kingdom of God on earth. They must take up arms (at least figuratively) if that's the only way to secure justice for themselves and others. Mystical insights, ideas, plans and reflections should forge action, or they are merely pretty thoughts.

Some have called Joan "the first Protestant," because she takes her cues for action from an internal source, putting her conscience above the church (the primacy of conscience was not affirmed until the Second Vatican Council), and because her response to her voices is so practical. Of course, she lived more than a hundred years before the Reformation began. But she is not content to leave everything for God to do. If God helps those who help themselves, then she's going to do her part.

Maybe that is somewhat Protestant. Protestants set a great deal of store by "God helps those who help themselves." When I was in the Catholic country of Brazil in the 1990s, I visited a favela in Rio de Janeiro. This slum was terribly unsanitary, with an open drainage ditch coming down the hill. The area reeked, and children were getting sick. The pipes lay rusting on the ground, awaiting installation. But the very Catholic people of this area preferred to spend six months of the year preparing floats and entries for the annual Carnival (Mardi Gras) parade rather than connecting up the new pipes. I don't mean to criticize the priorities of Brazilians, but, coming from the United States, which is so shaped by the Puritan work ethic, I confess I do find them strange.

The idea that God helps those who help themselves led some to believe that only the "deserving poor" should be helped. Of course, this is a misappropriation of the idea. (Who is to decide who is "deserving"?) This is not part of Joan's approach. She's no Norman Vincent Peale, but she is into "self-help."

BRING YOUR HAMMER

What people want out of life is usually not just handed to them, like a present or birthright. It has to be worked for. The Nike slogan, "Just do it," has definite merit. As the Elf-Help book *Take-Charge-of-Your-Life Therapy* puts it: "Don't accept the limitations of other people who claim things are undoable or unchangeable. If it's written in stone, bring your hammer and chisel."[12]

Optimism is the fuel of change. No one has ever effected change without having been convinced it could be done. *The Impossible Will Take a Little While: A Citizen's Guide to Hope in a Time of Fear* recommends adopting the "long view" and practicing patience: "In 'The Small Work in the Great Work,' the Reverend Victoria Safford advises us to 'plant ourselves at the gates of hope,' even in times or situations that would invite pessimism because 'with our lives we make our answers all the time, to this ravenous, beautiful, mutilated, gorgeous world.'"[13] That book's editor, Paul Rogat Loeb, recalls recent events that have taken aim at injustice, such as apartheid being brought down in South Africa by Archbishop Desmond Tutu and his outspoken supporters. Loeb chooses to begin the book's collection of inspiring essays and other contributions with a few verses from Nobel Prize–winning poet Seamus Heaney's "The Cure at Troy":

> *History says, Don't hope*
> *On this side of the grave.*
> *But then, once in a lifetime*
> *The longed-for tidal wave*
> *Of justice can rise up,*
> *And hope and history rhyme.*[14]

When Joan started toward Orléans, hope and history were about to rhyme.

FOR REFLECTION

1. What turns you to action? What motivates you to get out of bed each day? At what point do you "take up arms"?
2. Whose "permission" do you need to take a new direction, to start a new venture, to change your life? Who do you enlist in your cause?
3. Is being an activist in the Catholic tradition?
4. Would you have told the duke to leave his mistress when you were seeking his support?

CLOSING PRAYER

O God,

help me to take action against injustice

wherever I find it.

Wherever people are oppressed, hungry, without options,
hopeless,

let me bring freedom, food, choices and hope.

Let me join with others doing this.

I may not be able to eliminate the injustice,

but help me to do whatever I can.

In the end you're not counting on me to succeed,

but only to try.

Amen.

Notes

1. Twain, p. 20.
2. Twain, p. 448.
3. Siobhan Nash-Marshall, *Joan of Arc: A Spiritual Biography* (New York: Crossroad, 1999), p. 24.
4. Nash-Marshall, p. 25.
5. http://members.aol.com/hywebsite/private/joanofarc_quotes.html.
6. Polly Schoyer Brooks, *Beyond the Myth: The Story of Joan of Arc* (Boston: Houghton Mifflin, 1990), p. 26.
7. Brooks, p. 27.
8. Brooks, p. 32.
9. Brooks, p. 41.
10. Brooks, pp. 44–45.
11. Daniel L. Schutte, s.j., "What You Hear in the Dark," *Glory and Praise: Songs for Christian Assembly*, volume two (Phoenix: North American Liturgy Resources, 1980), p. 73.
12. *Take-Charge-of-Your-Life Therapy,* adapted from the bestseller *Life 101: Everything We Wish We Had Learned in School—But Didn't,* edited by Lisa O. Engelhardt, illustrated by R.W. Alley (St. Meinrad, Ind.: Abbey, 1995), no. 19.
13. Paul Rogat Loeb, *The Impossible Will Take a Little While: A Citizen's Guide to Hope in a Time of Fear* (New York: Basic, 2004), p. 9.
14. Seamus Heaney, "The Cure at Troy," as quoted in Loeb, p. 16.

DAY THREE

EXPANDING GENDER ROLES

"Entirely unofficially, Joan is raucously celebrated each year at Chicago's Gay Pride Parade as the patron saint of cross-dressers."
—"Odd Saint Fact," *Heaven Help Us*[1]

COMING TOGETHER IN THE SPIRIT

Joan is a proto-feminist, one who ignores the traditional role assigned to women. She never would have recognized the rhetoric of contemporary feminism or called herself a feminist, but clearly, as stated earlier, she marched to a different drummer. She is so focused on her mission of restoring France to the French that she has no patience for traditional roles or sexual games. She has chosen not just to take the road "less traveled by"[2] but to go where no woman has gone before.

The church today honors her as a virgin, not a virgin-and-martyr. (In the church's opinion she can't be a martyr because her martyrdom came at the hands of the church.) The issue of her virginity was an important point during her lifetime, a way others judged the veracity of what she was promoting, almost a magical sign. She herself saw virginity as a way of keeping herself free from any man's power to stop her. Twice (at Poitiers and Rouen) she submitted to physical examinations that confirmed her virginity; it was believed that a witch could not be a virgin. Having a pact with the devil implied sexual relations with him.[3]

The church still holds virginity in high regard, indicating a total devotion to God. Most of the women celebrated as saints in the church's liturgical calendar are virgins.

Joan's refusal to give up wearing men's clothes was judged the ultimate and visible sign of her refusal to submit to church authority. It sealed the court's verdict that she be put to death.

OPENING PRAYER

> God,
> in your image
> you created male and female,[4]
> and you saw your creation as "very good."[5]
> But with baptism in Christ,
> there is no longer male and female;[6]
> we are mutual heirs of the kingdom,
> equal children of our Father.
> Help us realize our intrinsic goodness,
> the demands of equality
> and the responsibility of our sex-edness.
> Amen.

RETREAT SESSION THREE

> "There are plenty of other women to do it."
>
> —Joan of Arc on "women's work"[7]

When the interrogators at the church court at Rouen asked Joan why she was not doing women's work, her answer was terse. Although she had spent the first seventeen years of her life doing housework, looking after livestock and spinning wool, she now saw a task only she could do, and she was going to do it.

When she was waiting for the dauphin's approval in Vaucouleurs, she exchanged her red peasant dress for a man's long tunic, long hose and leggings. (Later in battle, she would wear armor made of overlapping steel plates, "far more protective against arrows, crossbow bolts, or sword slashes than chain mail, but it was so heavy—often weighing sixty pounds—that a knight had to be helped onto his horse."[8]) To fit in better, she cut her long black hair. (The few other things we know about her appearance were that she had brown eyes and a swarthy complexion, a good figure and a lovely voice.[9]) It has been said that a woman's hair is her crowning glory, and Joan was probably no exception to this cultural view. To cut her hair "in a boyish fashion, short above the ears"[10] was a major sign of her commitment to this military venture on which she was about to embark. But her cut hair would better accommodate the shallow steel battle helmet she wore as part of the armor.[11]

Two banners for battle were crafted for her. Joan's personal standard had Jesus as the king of heaven seated on a rainbow, flanked by the Archangels Michael and Gabriel. The company's pennon had an Annunciation scene, with Gabriel giving the Virgin Mary a double lily, a twofold symbol of France and of chastity.[12]

The story of her sword has shades of the legendary King Arthur's Excalibur. She sent for a certain sword that she thought was near the altar of St. Catherine's Chapel at Fierbois, where she had prayed on route to Chinon. (Whether it was buried or she had seen it unconsciously is not known. St. Catherine's was a favorite pilgrimage center for released prisoners of war, who often left behind swords, shields and armor as votive offerings to the saint.[13]) Surprisingly, the sword Joan had predicted would be there was found there. When the rust was brushed away, five crosses were visible on the blade, just as Joan had predicted.[14]

Joan's choice of clothing was out of necessity, not personal preference. Her clothes were very practical for horseback riding, at which she was soon adept. She also picked her clothes to blend in, avoid attention and, most importantly, discourage rape. Men's clothes were much harder for someone else to remove forcibly. Joan's clothing became a point of obsession for the judges at Rouen.[15] They were hung up on the words of Deuteronomy: "A woman shall not wear / the clothes of a man, / nor a man / the clothes of a woman. / For abominable / in the eyes of God / are those who do."[16]

Even at her trial the interrogators tried to blackmail her by offering her the opportunity to attend Easter Mass in prison if she would forsake male dress. She initially agreed but soon "relapsed." Most likely, it was after "someone approached her secretly at night…and tried to take her by force."[17] In fact, she was so unnerved by the attack of this "great lord" that she immediately resumed male dress.

On the other hand, some say she went back to wearing men's clothes only because the guards took her female dress away from her.[18] The guards may have wanted her to renege on her promise and were trying to get her in trouble. Obviously, someone had to have provided the male dress.

As for rape, one recent movie speculates that she saw her sister Catherine raped in a raid on Domrémy. Most experts find little support for this contention. Certainly, Joan seems to have taken great care not to be an object of sexual desire.

Her father had dreamed that Joan would go away with the soldiers, fearing she would be considered a camp follower and turn to prostitution. He told her brothers to drown her if this turned out to be true and added that he would do it himself if they wouldn't. (This story says a lot about proscribed male and female roles at this time.)

But Joan's first supporter, the young knight Jean Metz, who often slept beside the fully clothed woman in the open fields or deserted barns, said that "at first they [he and other knights and squires] were tempted to make sexual advances but quickly realized that Joan was not that sort of girl."[19]

Joan had the power to get men to follow her, but it wasn't because she flaunted her sexuality.

A MASCULINE WOMAN

To call someone a "Masculine Woman!" was a medieval slur,[20] and it was sometimes hurled at her. Was Joan a lesbian? The issue was first advanced publicly by Victoria Sackville-West in a 1936 book,[21] based on some of the testimony at the nullification trial. Charlotte Boucher, who would have been nine at the time, and two other women said they "slept with" Joan at Orléans. This is easily explained, however, by that fact that, when a company of soldiers was billeted in a house where there weren't enough beds for everyone, Joan would always be placed with the little girls or hostess of the house, rather than with the men. Since Joan's male bodyguard, Jean d'Aulon, frequently slept in the same room with her, the women were with her to safeguard her from the man. The bulk of the girls-turned-women's testimony was about how chaste Joan was. Her sleeping with her sister as a child proves nothing, as that was the common practice among country families.

What were her relations with other women? Once Joan chased away a "wanton woman" who was following the army. She was "counseling her with gentleness and charity not to be found again in the company of men-at-arms, or she herself, Joan, would have to take measures against her."[22] She also brushed aside Catherine de la Rochelle, who "claimed to have access to 'the high secrets of Our

Lord God,'"[23] as part of the religious fringe. This may seem surprising in light of the fact that mystical experience was the basis for her own mission. But after spending two nights with Catherine at Montfaucon-en-Berry (later named Villequiers), Joan failed to see her "White Lady covered in gold" who had promised that the king would find treasure that he could use to fund his army.[24] She told Catherine to go home and tend to her family.

Most other women Joan met went out of their way to look out after her. The three Joans she came into contact with when she was kept imprisoned in the tower of the keep of Beaurevoir—Joan of Bar, Joan of Béthune and Joan of Luxembourg—tried to alleviate her hardship, although they did offer her material to make a new dress.[25] Isabelle of Portugal, the wife of Philip the Good, who visited her at Beaulieu, probably got her moved to Beaurevoir, a more suitable residence for the prisoner. There, Joan of Luxembourg, the aunt of the man who had captured her, had instructed the guards to leave her unmolested. None of these women claimed intimacy with her.

Judging by the evidence, it would not seem that Joan was a lesbian. Apparently, she was too focused on her mission to be distracted by sexual relations with men or women.

WARRIOR ARCHETYPE

Joan's major gender-bending was not in the adoption of male clothes, but of a male archetype. Carl Jung suggested that there are psychological archetypes (or patterns) in the human personality, part of our collective unconscious. "Warrior" is the archetype that comes to the fore when a person fights to protect others, defends the castle or stands up against unfair authority. Archangel Michael is an exemplar of this archetype. It used to be one of the prime archetypes associated with men.[26]

Now that women are freer to shape their identities, more women let their "warrior" archetype out. Women are often in the forefront of justice movements like Mairead Corrigan and the "Peace Women" of Northern Ireland, prominent a few years ago. Even physically frail women, such as Blessed Mother Teresa of Calcutta, can be tigers when it comes to defending the poorest of the poor. Back in Joan's day, however, when women were to be subservient, Joan's warrior persona was a real shocker.

FOR REFLECTION

1. What is the value of virginity today? Do women and men see this differently?

2. If Joan had been raped, would it make her any less of a saint? Would the same be true if she had been a lesbian?

3. What's your reaction to gay pride parades, gay and lesbian information centers, cross-dressers and music performers who affect androgyny or imitate the opposite sex?

4. Do you think sexual identity is inherited or learned?

5. What brings out your warrior persona?

CLOSING PRAYER

God,
may we learn from Joan's example
how to guard the treasure that each of us is.
Single or married, religious or lay,
all are called to chastity.
May we value ourselves
as highly as you do
and be fitting mirrors of your image.
Amen.

Notes

1. Alice La Plante and Clare La Plante, *Heaven Help Us: The Worrier's Guide to the Patron Saints* (New York: Dell, 1999), p. 56.
2. Robert Frost, "The Road Not Taken," *Robert Frost: Selected Poems* (New York: Gramercy, 1992), p. 163.
3. Brooks, pp. 45–46.
4. Genesis 1:27.
5. Genesis 1:31.
6. Galatians 3:28.
7. http://www.stjoan-center.com/quotable.
8. Brooks, p. 48.
9. Brooks, p. 18.
10. Brooks, p. 34.
11. Pernoud and Clin, p. 225.
12. "St. Joan's Battle Standard, Pennon and Banner," available at www.stjoancenter.com/topics/standard.html.
13. Brooks, p. 39.
14. Brooks, pp. 48–49.
15. Pernoud and Clin, p. 123.
16. Deuteronomy 22:5, as used in Richard Einhorn, *Voices of Light: An Oratorio Inspired by the Film The Passion of Joan of Arc* (Sony Classical, 1994).
17. Pernoud and Clin, p. 132.
18. Pernoud and Clin, p. 132.
19. Brooks, p. 38.
20. Einhorn, p. 15.
21. Victoria Sackville-West, *Saint Joan of Arc* (London: Cobden-Sanderson, 1936).
22. Pernoud and Clin, p. 226.
23. Pernoud and Clin, p. 200.
24. Pernoud and Clin, pp. 79–80.
25. Pernoud and Clin, p. 93.
26. See Robert Moore and Douglas Gillette, *King, Warrior, Magician, Lover: Rediscovering the Archetypes of the Mature Masculine* (New York: HarperSanFrancisco, 1991), or Robert Bly, *Iron John: A Book About Men* (New York: Vintage, 1992).

DAY FOUR

TRUSTING

IN

GOD

"The phenomenon of Jeanne d'Arc—the voices from God who told her she must expel the English and have the Dauphin crowned King, the quality that dominated those who would normally have despised her, the strength that raised the siege of Orléans and carried the Dauphin to Reims—belongs to no category. Perhaps it can only be explained as the answer called forth by an exigent historic need. The moment required her and she rose. Her strength came from the fact that in her were combined for the first time the old religious faith and the new force of patriotism. God spoke to her through the voices of St. Catherine, St. Michael, and St. Margaret, but what He commanded was not chastity nor humility nor the life of the spirit but political action to rescue her country from foreign tyrants."

Mary (Mother of Jesus)

—Barbara W. Tuchman, *A Distant Mirror*[1]

COMING TOGETHER IN THE SPIRIT

Joan's voices gave her confidence that she could win military victories, but her trust was not in her own power to influence people or change the course of history. Neither was her trust in her companions nor in their military strategies. It was in God alone. "I place trust in God, my creator, in all things, I love him with all my heart," she kept saying.[2]

Her trust in God led her to the most surprising victories over the English. Later, it sustained her in imprisonment and even unto the stake.

Her trust was open-hearted, born out of prayer, and is among the easiest lessons of her life for us to understand—and perhaps the hardest to emulate.

OPENING PRAYER

God,
you led Joan to great victories
just as you let the youth David
bring down the Philistine Goliath.[3]
You write straight
with what I see as crooked lines.
Give me the trust I need
to realize that you are in charge
of my life and our world.
Amen.

RETREAT SESSION FOUR

"I fear nothing, for God is with me."

—Joan of Arc[4]

"Jehanne...the Maid sends you news from these parts: that in one week she has chased the English out of all the places that they held along the Loire river, either by assault or otherwise, in which encounters many English were killed and captured and she has routed them in a pitched battle. A brother of the Earl of Suffolk's and Glasdale were killed.

"I promise and assure you [that we will take possession] of all the cities that must belong to [our] holy realm...in spite of all opposition.

"So God, King of Heaven, wills it; and so it has been revealed
by the Maid."

—Joan's letter after the victory at Orléans[5]

On March 22, 1429, Joan dictated her ultimatum to the king of
England, which is known as the "Letter to the English." It begins in
the name of Jesus and Mary, and demands that the English king, the
duke of Bedford, the earl of Suffolk and Sir Thomas Scales

> render your account to the King of Heaven. Surrender to the
> Maid, who is sent here from God, the King of Heaven, the keys
> to all of the good cities that you have taken and violated in
> France. She has come here from God to proclaim the blood royal.
> She is entirely ready to make peace, if you are willing to settle
> accounts with her, provided that you give up France and pay for
> having occupied her. And those among you, archers, compan-
> ions-at-arms, gentlemen, and others who are before the city of
> Orléans, go back to your own countries, for God's sake.... If you
> do not wish to believe this message from God through the Maid,
> then wherever we find you we will strike you there, and make
> great uproar[,] greater than any made in France for a thousand
> years.... And believe firmly that the King of Heaven will send the
> Maid more force than you will ever know how to achieve.... [W]e
> shall see who has better right from the king of Heaven....[6]

If ever there was psychological war, this was it. Her firm conviction
that she would succeed began to intimidate the English, who were
already spooked by rumors they had been hearing about her. At
Tours she collected men and equipment, and helped prepare the
army by urging them to go to confession. She forbade blasphemy,
pillage and oaths.[7] She was definitely a different kind of general,
with different priorities.

When she got near Orléans, she was on the south bank of the Loire, which was controlled by the French, but Orléans is on the north shore. Luckily, right after she arrived, the winds turned to blow from the west and allowed the boats to sail upriver to Orléans, which the soldiers took as a sign of God's favor. On horseback Joan entered the city, inspiring confidence in the citizens who had endured a seven-month siege. When more troops marshaled by the king arrived, there was a small skirmish which turned into a French victory when she got there, securing the bastide of Saint-Loop, on the old Roman road close to the Burgundy Gate. This was really Joan's first encounter with war, and she "grieved mightily...she wept for the men who died without confession." She fired off two more letters warning the English. Then she blocked an English retreat from one of the islands in the river.[8]

On May 7 an arrow penetrated Joan's breastplate. It must not have been too deep because the arrow was removed, the usual remedy of olive oil and bacon fat was applied, and she quickly returned to the assault of the fortress of Tourelles. She had the motherly instinct to insist that her troops get some food, wine and rest. Later, she grabbed her standard, and the men rallied around her to fight. Tourelles fell, so the French could cross the bridge and go into the city. The next day was Sunday. By insisting on a ban on fighting on Sundays and feast days (according to the old rules of chivalry), the two armies stood very close to each other without touching for an hour. The English could no longer stand the tension and withdrew. Orléans had been totally liberated.[9]

Between May 9 and 21, she engaged in a pitched battle at Patay, where the English lost two thousand men but the French lost few.

She then convinced the reluctant dauphin to come to Reims, and she and her army fought their way there. On July 17, 1429, in the Reims cathedral, the dauphin was crowned King Charles VII of France, with Joan standing next to him.

After these successes, Joan experienced failures, such as the September 6 defeat at the Saint-Honoré Gate in Paris. The final blow was being captured at Compiègne because, in protecting a French retreat, she became isolated on the battlefield. A drawbridge to the city had been drawn up, leaving her outside, and she was pulled off her horse. Her predicament felt like a betrayal—whether it was deliberate or not, who knows.[10]

It is said that Joan never used her sword in battle. She held it and her standard high to rally her troops. After each battle or skirmish she would comfort the wounded and mourn for the dead of both sides in the field. Some say her role was more cheerleader than general, but actually Joan was involved in the nitty-gritty of the campaigns.

Through it all, Joan kept her trust in God. "I fear nothing, for God is with me," she had said at Vaucouleurs before she saw her first blood on the battlefield. She held true to that—in war and later in imprisonment.

JUST WAR

It's hard to envision the kind of war which Joan fought. Her rules of engagement, like warning the enemy and Sunday truces, seem quaint to us, far removed from the nuclear threat and 9/11, attacks on food convoys in Iraq, terrorist threats against Wall Street, anthrax letters, deadly explosions in Madrid and shoe bombers.

But Joan's kind of war does meet the criteria of a "just war," the traditional teaching of the church and one recently rearticulated by the U.S. bishops.[11] The church teaches that lethal force may be used if all of the following conditions are met: if there is a just cause—

to correct some grave evil, like aggression or the massive violation of the rights of whole populations; if one party's wrongs significantly outweigh the wrongs suffered by the other party (comparative justice); if the war is pursued by legitimate public authorities; if the war is pursued with the "right intention"—only to correct the evil; if there is a probability of success (arms are not to be used in a futile cause or if disproportionate measures or losses, especially of lives, are likely); if the overall destruction is proportionate to the good to be achieved; if all peaceful alternatives have been exhausted so that war is a "last resort."

Joan's French were an occupied people, subjected to a war that had gone on a hundred years. Their liberation was an act of justice (unlike the church's pronouncement on the military actions of the United States of late). An ever more complicated world makes it more difficult to determine just who the bad guys are.

"What, Me Worry?"

Alfred E. Neuman, a creation of *Mad* magazine, may have uttered this phrase as a symptom of his stupidity. There are indeed things we should be worrying about: keeping our jobs in tough economic times; protecting our kids; doing the best we can for aging parents; choosing the right courses of action for our country in war and peace. The list goes on and on.

But worry usually just spins our wheels fruitlessly. The better option is to follow Joan's principle: Put our trust in God. Who else has the answers, the overarching plan, the big arms to embrace us in love? As the Serenity Prayer, linked to Reinhold Niebuhr and adopted by Alcoholics Anonymous, says,

God, grant me
Serenity to accept the things I cannot change,

Courage to change the things I can,
And wisdom to know the difference.[12]

As Carol Ann Morrow notes, trust must start simply in order to grow: "If you can't begin by believing in God's love for you, begin by believing that the earth's surface can support your weight while gravity keeps you from floating off. In the simplest actions, you reveal considerable trust."[13] Trust grows only if you work at it. Trusting God can develop only after you first learn to trust a friend, a teacher, a spouse, a child.

God is always there to hold us up, just as fathers teach daughters to swim, just as mothers hold onto their sons as they ice skate for the first time. Good parents always teach their children to develop their talents, take risks and stretch out—even if the outcome of such efforts is uncertain. God, too, is always calling us beyond ourselves, asking us to take a risk. Trust is accepting the loving embrace of God and realizing we are always standing on large shoulders.

FOR REFLECTION

1. Why did Joan feel it necessary to warn the English?
2. From where did this peasant girl get her confidence?
3. Did her voices reveal military strategies?
4. How do you apply the "just war" principles to Joan's Hundred Years' War and to the military actions of today?
5. Can you trust in God too much?

CLOSING PRAYER

God,
I place my hand in yours,
knowing that you will always

look out for me.
Let me be a reliable anchor
where my family, colleagues at work,
neighbors and others may be able to
place their trust
and never be disappointed.
Amen.

Notes

1. Barbara W. Tuchman, *A Distant Mirror: The Calamitous 14th Century* (New York: Knopf, 1979), p. 588.
2. http://www.stjoan-center.com/quotable.
3. 1 Samuel 17.
4. http://www.stjoan-center.com/quotable.
5. Einhorn, p. 15.
6. Pernoud and Clin, pp. 34–35.
7. Pernoud and Clin, p. 38.
8. Pernoud and Clin, pp. 42–46.
9. Pernoud and Clin, pp. 48–49.
10. Pernoud and Clin, p. 87.
11. United States Conference of Catholic Bishops, *The Harvest of Justice Is Sown in Peace* (Washington, D.C.: USCCB, 1993).
12. Foley and Normile, p. 206.
13. Carol Ann Morrow, *Trust-in-God Therapy* (St. Meinrad, Ind.: Abbey, 1998), no. 16.

DAY FIVE

OVERCOMING
BETRAYAL

"And for all reward, the French King, whom she had crowned, stood supine and indifferent..."

—Mark Twain, *Joan of Arc*[1]

COMING TOGETHER IN THE SPIRIT

Prisoners of war know a peculiar loneliness, despair and sense of betrayal. They fault themselves for failure. They blame anyone who could have rescued them but didn't. They rail at God for their fate and worry about what lies ahead for them. Not knowing what's in their future is the worst part of their imprisonment.

American prisoners of the Vietnam War experienced all of these emotions, points out now-Senator John McCain, who spent years imprisoned in the infamous "Hanoi Hilton." Unlike Joan of Arc, imprisoned alone, the Vietnam POWs had some comfort through contact with one another. But without letters from home or real news from America, they had no idea if anyone remembered or cared about them or was doing anything to secure their release.

Recent political prisoners like Václav Havel of Czechoslovakia and Nelson Mandela of South Africa have spoken of how they occupied their years in prison. Havel was already a renowned dramatist and poet before becoming a political essayist arguing for intellectual freedom against the communists. He was subjected to constant government surveillance and harassment. During his longest prison stay of four years, he wrote *Largo Desolato,* a play about a political writer who fears being sent back to prison. Mandela, a lawyer who worked with the African National Congress organizing against the apartheid system of segregation in his country, spent twenty-eight years in prison. He says he most missed seeing the sun and listening to music (especially African choral music and classical European music). What kept him strong was maintaining the discipline of his athletic youth, with regular hours for rising and sleeping, an eating regimen and morning exercises. He spent his time working behind the scenes for democracy and equality.

These leaders' unswerving devotion to their political ideals impressed others. In the end, Havel became a leading figure in the Velvet Revolution of 1989, which nonviolently overthrew the communists. In December of that year, he was unanimously voted president of the Federal Assembly of Czechoslovakia and retained the title in the first free elections of the country in 1990. When the country split, he was elected the first president of the Czech Republic in 1993 and reelected in 1998. Mandela became South Africa's first democratically elected State President, serving from 1994 to 1999.

Luckily, most of us don't experience the years of privation these men did. But we may know prisons of other sorts: abusive relationships, financial struggles, the limits imposed by racism or sexism, lack of education or opportunities.

Joan of Arc's particular pain lay in the betrayal that kept her in prison: Charles VII, whose crowning as king of France she had personally seen to, refused to ransom her or make any attempt to free her. Neither did any of her fellow soldiers or noble new friends.

OPENING PRAYER

God,

you allowed Joan to be taken by her enemies

and forsaken by her friends.

The times I have been betrayed seem small

in comparison, but they hurt all the same.

In my pain and abandonment,

let me learn to abandon myself to you.

You alone are my true friend.

Amen.

RETREAT SESSION FIVE

"I fear nothing, except treason."

—Joan of Arc, speaking to a friend from Domrémy[2]

"By my martin."

—Joan of Arc[3]

In December 1429 Joan and her family were invited to the royal court. Joan had not asked that the king make her a knight, but wanted recognition for her brothers. At Jargeau, Charles ennobled her and her family, his letter stating that he was

> Wishing to give thanks for the multiple and striking benefits of divine grandeur that have been accorded us through the agency of the Maid, Jeanne d'Ay de Domrémy...considering also the praiseworthy, graceful, and useful services already rendered by the aforesaid Joan the Maid in every way, to us and to our kingdom, which we hope to pursue in the future.[4]

The king granted the family the rare privilege of making their title inheritable through both the male and female lines. It was an act of gratitude—and farewell. Joan's nobility meant she could raise armies of her own, and no longer needed his permission. But that privilege had its downside: She had to maintain her army. Charles was beginning to cut her loose.

Joan's voices had told her on Easter Sunday 1430, at Melun, that she would be captured by the enemy "before the feast of St. John" (meaning the nativity of John the Baptist on June 24), "that this had to be, that she should not be surprised but take everything in good part, and that God would help her." The forewarning of her destiny was repeated "several times and nearly every day."[5] The prospect of capture was not devastating to her since usually a ransom was set by the captors and eventually paid by one's friends. Such had been the experience of some whom she fought alongside.

On May 23, 1429, her doublet was seized and she was pulled from her horse to the ground. Lionel de Wandomme had seized her as she and a few of her men somehow got shut out when the drawbridge to the city gate closed. Lionel, sometimes called "the Bastard," was a lieutenant of John of Luxembourg, whose prisoner she became. "The Burgundian and English partisans were very joyous, more than if they had taken five hundred combatants, for they did not fear or dread either captains or any other war chief as much as they had up to that day this maid," commented the Burgundian chronicler Enguerrand de Monstrelet.[6]

Nowadays, it's taken for granted that prisoners of war have the right—and even the duty—to try to escape. It is unclear if, when Joan was captured, she ever actually agreed to "[s]urrender to me and tender faith," meaning to give her promise not to escape, the ritual of surrender in fifteenth-century warfare. She supposedly replied, "I have sworn and tendered faith to another than you, and I shall keep my oath."[7] Therefore, later when she attempted escapes, she was not breaking her promise.

THE INTERVENTION OF WOMEN

In every age, swearing seems to be a part of a soldier's life. She often referred to the English as "Godons," a slang term for them at the time because the French thought all the English said was the expletive "goddamn." When Joan was vexed on the field of battle, she was heard to say, "By my martin," a very mild form of swearing. No one seems to have recorded what she said when she was captured, however. It might have been much stronger than that. What is known is that she was disappointed because they were in the midst of a retreat, anyway, and her preference was always for moving forward, not backward. On top of a retreat, to have been seized must have really unsettled her.

With her brother Pierre, her steward Jean d'Aulon and his brother Poton the Burgundian, she was taken temporarily to the fortress of Clairoix, then to the castle of Beaulieu-lès-Fontaines. Then she was separated from her brother and steward and transferred to the castle of Beaurevoir. Her better lodgings may have been urged by the wife of Duke Philip the Good of Burgundy, the savvy and diplomatic Isabel of Portugal, who was the sister of King Henry the Explorer of Portugal. Isabel met briefly with Joan of Arc and seemed sympathetic to her.

It was at Beaurevoir that three other Joans enter her story: Joan of Béthune, who was married to John of Luxembourg; Joan of Bar, who was Joan of Béthune's daughter from her first marriage; and Joan of Luxembourg, who was John's aunt. These women made Joan's captivity easier, and much is made of their roles in the many films about Joan. She often seems to have brought out the attention, sympathy and ministrations of other women.

Over the next seven months, there were negotiations for her ransom. In the end, she was not ransomed but bought for a "sale price" of ten thousand pounds paid by the English crown. Actually, John of Luxembourg and his lord, Duke Philip, were not anxious to hand her over to the English and the University of Paris faction led by Bishop Pierre Cauchon. Joan said at her trial, "The lady of Luxembourg [John's aunt] asked my lord of Luxembourg that I not be delivered to the English." It was at this time that the "very ancient"[8] (as the sixty-seven-year-old was described by chronicler Monstrelet) Joan of Luxembourg had just inherited the titles, lands and wealth of her brother, Philip of Brabant. She had willed her nephew John the bulk of her estate, passing over his older brother, Lord Enghien. John would not have wanted to jeopardize his inheritance by going against his aunt.

"Joan's death, as such, teaches us as much as her life does, For Joan was betrayed. There can be no doubt about this. Charles of Valois may not personally have delivered her to the Anglo-Burgundians, but he was certainly glad that she was gone,"[9] according to Siobhan Nash-Marshall.

Joan could not read, could not dictate letters and was deprived of the solace of Mass during much of her imprisonment. She appears to have spent the time at Beaurevoir praying, pacing and worrying about the fate of her comrades-in-arms. The other three Joans offered her women's clothes or the material to make some. Joan said at her trial that their offer tempted her: "I would have dressed in women's clothes more willingly at the request of these women than of any other woman who might be in France, except for my queen."[10] But she did not yield even to them.

Twice Joan attempted escape: the first, after shutting her guard in the tower and trying to walk out "between two pieces of wood" but getting stopped by the porter; the second, a more desperate attempt referred to as the "leap of Beaurevoir," when she jumped sixty feet from the keep's tower but was immediately caught. (Somehow she suffered only minor injuries.) Was the latter a suicide attempt? It occurred after Bishop Cauchon's visit when "I knew that I had been sold to the English, and I would have preferred to die rather than to be in the hands of the English, my enemies."[11] Attempting suicide was among the accusations brought against her at her trial. Most people excuse her flinging herself out of the window as due to her youth and a belief in her own invincibility.

LONELINESS IN PRISON

Since Joan left no diary, no one knows for sure what she felt in prison. Scared, certainly, and afraid of rape, since she was in the hands of men. Worried, undoubtedly, as her future and the success of her mission were in doubt. Lonely, for sure. Despairing, possibly.

As she was being transferred to Beaulieu, she was allowed to pray at a priory dedicated to Saint Margaret (one of her voices) near the village of Élincourt. That must have given her some comfort as she began her imprisonment. After her jump from the tower, "I had comfort from St. Catherine [another of her voices] who told me to confess myself and ask pardon from God for having jumped and that without fail the people of Compiègne would have help before the feast of St. Martin in the winter. And so I began to return to health; I began to eat and soon I was healed."[12] Indeed, Compiègne was liberated on October 28. It seems that prayer and her voices were sustaining her through this trying time.

In prayer, we too can hear of God's constant love for us, despite our sufferings, disappointments and betrayals. Prayer opens us to accept that God knows more than we do and has a plan for us.

In the prisons imposed on us and the ones we impose on ourselves, we need to reach out to others, like the "other Joans" with whom we come into contact. We need to see which prisons are self-imposed and find open doors wherever we can. What did those other Joans do for her? They probably secured for her safer living conditions, better accommodations and food. They listened to her and occasionally let a priest visit her to give her the sacraments. What probably intrigued them about her was that she was one woman who was not defined by the men in her life, as they were, but had set out on her own path.

As to the matter of those who betrayed her, it is possible that Joan's friends may have assumed, because of her power and God's protection, no harm would befall her. When she was captured, many people refused to believe the reports. In regions sympathetic to the French cause, the clergy ordered prayers for her liberation. Her growing myth made them believe that no prison could hold her since her work was not done.

Charles VII's abandonment of her was certainly Joan's most cutting betrayal. Her life's mission was to have Charles crowned king and to drive the English out of his country. Clearly, Joan pursued this course convinced that it was God's will, but Charles seemed to have been equally confident of this fact. We do not know what gratitude, if any, he felt toward God, but his behavior toward Joan was no less than perfidious. Her suffering and sacrifice must have seemed to him no more than what any good subject owed to a sovereign, and he was determined that he himself, not Joan, would be the hero of this drama. Joan, somehow, comes to terms with this, and begins to see it all as part of God's plan for her and for France.

FOR REFLECTION

1. Can you think of other prisoners who have found their way through their darkness?
2. What is imprisoning (or limiting) you?
3. If you had forewarning of your destiny, how would you proceed?
4. Was Joan a political pawn? Was John of Luxembourg forced to turn her over? Were the "other Joans" torn by allegiances beyond their control?
5. How would you survive in prison? Do you draw your strength from faith or from external sources?
6. Aid organizations like Amnesty International focus attention on those imprisoned for their political beliefs. How can you help a criminal or political prisoner today?
7. Do you think Joan tried to commit suicide? Why or why not?

CLOSING PRAYER

> God,
> just as you sustained Joan
> through disappointment, betrayal and imprisonment,
> I know that you are protecting me, too.
> Let me never betray those who look up to me.
> Let me forgive others who wrong me,
> remembering how you forgave those who nailed you to the
>   cross.
> Let me be a rock on which others can lean
> in their times of hardship.
> When all seems bleak,
> send me signs of your presence,
> signs as simple as rainbows and smiles.
> Amen.

Notes

1. Twain, p. 21.
2. http://www.stjoan-center.com/quotable.
3. http://members.aol.com/hywebsite/private/joanofarc_quotes.html.
4. Pernoud and Clin, p. 81.
5. George H. Tavard, *The Spiritual Way of St. Jeanne d'Arc* (Collegeville, Minn.: Liturgical, 1998), p. 135, 137.
6. Pernoud and Clin, p. 88.
7. Pernoud and Clin, pp. 87–88.
8. Pernoud and Clin, pp. 93, 191.
9. Nash-Marshall, p. 172.
10. Pernoud and Clin, p. 93.
11. Pernoud and Clin, pp. 92, 96.
12. Pernoud and Clin, p. 96.

DAY SIX

BATTLING

THE

CHURCH

"The Charges: Heretic, Apostate, Sorceress, Idolater, Cross-Dresser

"Joan was tried by an ecclesiastical court, and so the charges against her were all religious in their nature. One way of thinking of Joan's hearing is that it was the first of the great witchcraft trials. The fear of witches was entering the European air at the end of the fourteenth century, and it was connected to anxieties about class and particularly gender mobility. By connecting Joan's military victories with witchcraft, the English were able to justify their losses—all the more humiliating, since they were losses to a woman."

—Mary Gordon, *Joan of Arc*[1]

COMING TOGETHER IN THE SPIRIT

The trial was the highlight of Joan's life, and the dramatic pivot for most of the novels, movies and plays about her. We have a lot of primary information about the trial because the court records were preserved. They were written first in French, the language both the questioners and Joan used, and then translated into Latin.

With her hands bound, Joan rode from Beaurevoir to Rouen but was allowed to stop and pray at several abbeys and chapels along the way. On this trip she probably crossed the estuary of the Somme River by boat and saw the sea (the English Channel, beyond which lay the homeland of her enemies) for the first time in her life. (The accompanying knights and their fifty horses likely crossed by the bridge at Abbeville.)

She arrived at the castle of Rouen, the fortress of Bouvreuil, on December 23, 1430. (What people see today in Rouen is not exactly where she was imprisoned and tried, even though it is now named for her. "What is today called the Joan of Arc Tower represents the heavily restored remains of the ancient keep, not the site of her detention."[2] But certainly her jail cell and courtroom were nearby within the confines of Bouvreuil.) Built a century before by King Philip II Augustus, Bouvreuil was then the residence of Richard Beauchamp, the earl of Warwick, who was the guardian of the young English King Henry VI.

The five-month trial had a number of parts: preliminary investigations and interrogations of Joan; public sessions in the main part of the castle at Rouen, in which Joan remained eloquent; the sessions in her prison cell, where she seems confused; and the brief "relapse trial," which condemns her. Joan plays better to a crowd and is more intimidated when the judge, assessors (who acted like a jury to advise the chief judge and vice-inquisitor), interrogators and recorders are only feet away, invading her space—miserable as her jail cell is.

Trial defendants in those days were not allowed defense attorneys. Rarely were they ever cautioned against self-incrimination. The assessors acted as prosecutors as well. Her friends, supporters and witnesses favoring her side of the story were not allowed into the trial—much less the city of Rouen—which was securely under English control.

Joan's chief judge and interrogator was Bishop Pierre Cauchon (whose name appropriately enough translates to "pig" in English).

He had a degree in law and had become rector of the University of Paris after a distinguished teaching career there. After allying himself with the right parties in the church and civil uproar of the times, he was named bishop and count of Beauvais. Now he was in exile from his diocese because he had supported the English and Beauvais had gone over to the French. He was then sixty years old; Joan was nineteen at the time of her trial.

This is a classic confrontation between an old man and a young girl, between a renowned scholar and a simple peasant, between reason and passion. Joan starts with the edge—she truly believes God is on her side. But the questions are unremitting and repetitive; her voices desert her and she flounders.

Nowadays there's a tendency to see Cauchon "as a sincere and educated cleric with high if somewhat rigid professional standards, for whom Joan the Maid and her supporters embodied everything from which he wished to save his country."[3] Cauchon wanted the trial to be technically correct, but his zeal makes him commit what today we would call "reversible errors." Even if his reputation is rehabilitated, Cauchon is clearly the villain in Joan's story.

Do we ever face villains like Cauchon who embody the power of the church and society? Yes, of course. Those parents who insisted that the priests who had abused their children be removed from ministry know the power of an intransigent church that changed only after a bishops' conference reluctantly decided in favor of protecting children. Women who ask that their roles in the church be expanded, perhaps to include ordination to the diaconate or priesthood, face implacable resistance to even hearing their arguments, despite the church's urgent need today for more deacons and priests. Divorced people who cannot prove in a marriage tribunal that their marriage was invalid, or those who think theirs was valid but that they themselves have failed, see a church without pity or forgiveness. In the greater society, those who defend the rights of criminal and political prisoners know the difficulty of getting people to listen, even in the American legal system, supposedly predisposed to a presumption of innocence. Those fighting for halfway houses or the rights of the mentally ill encounter resistance, and those suggesting that suspected terrorists deserve trials before imprisonment are shouted down.

Anyone who has ever spoken truth to power can relate to Joan. When the case seems stacked against you, how do you proceed? How did Joan?

OPENING PRAYER

Dear God,
you always promised to be with us during our trials.
Joan's "trial" was literally a trial.
She showed more courage in her trial
than when she was struggling on bloody battlefields.
You helped her to stand tall
and gave her the words to impress the learned.
But then she had to deal with the silence of God,
the dark night of the soul.
That desolation of spiritual emptiness
is the hardest obstacle we face
in our journey toward you.
Preserve us in our dark times
with our spirits intact.
Amen.

Retreat Session Six

> "So long as she [the church] does not command anything impossible to do.... Yes, so long as Our Lord is served first."
>
> —Joan, when asked about obeying the Church Militant[4]

Before Joan is presented to the court on February 21, 1431, information has been gathered at Domrémy and Vaucouleurs from those who knew her.

The inquest into her habits and virtue that was undertaken in her homeland failed to produce compelling evidence against her. Having interrogated twelve or fifteen witnesses at Domrémy and in five or six neighboring parishes, Cauchon's representative Nicolas Bailly "had found nothing about Joan that he would not wish to find about his own sister."[5]

Another examination of her virginity (similar to the one at Poitiers) had been conducted in January 1430, under the auspices of Anne of Burgundy, duchess of Bedford. It, too, revealed Joan to be a virgin. This dispels insinuations that she is a wanton, disreputable woman, consorting freely with soldiers, and adds credence to her claim that she is on a mission from God. Again her virginity is viewed as proof of her sincerity and dedication.

Anne of Burgundy may also have forbidden the guards at Rouen to molest Joan. She was kept in leg irons and at night these were connected to a peg in the floor. A royal squire, John Grey, assisted by John Berwoit and William Talbot, had primary responsibility for her. They had to swear on a Bible that they would be vigilant and not allow anyone in to see her who had not been approved by Cauchon or Beauchamp. "[F]ive Englishmen of the lowest rank"[6] were also employed to keep her under surveillance, three of whom slept in her cell at night and the other two outside the door. The principal notary at her trial, Guillaume Manchon, reported that Joan feared that her captors would do her some violence at night. One or two times she complained to Cauchon, the subinquisitor and Master Nicolas Loiseleur (a canon of the Rouen cathedral) that one of her guards wished to violate her.

But the problems of her physical restraints and threats "must have seemed inconsequential compared to the mental torture to which Joan had to submit: the mockery of the guards, the hostile shouts, the obscenities and insults whenever she appeared in the courtyard of the castle."[7]

Since she was on trial for being a heretic, she should have been kept in an ecclesiastical prison, guarded by women. But instead she was treated as a prisoner of war, guarded by soldiers. Cauchon recognized this legal inconsistency, but claimed that since the three keys to the lock of her prison cell were held only by himself, by the promoter (prosecutor) Jean d'Estivet or the designated vice-inquisitor Jean L'Maître, and by Cardinal Henry Beaufort (bishop of Winchester)—all of whom were clerics—Joan was never out of church hands.

There was an irregularity with the vice-inquisitor as well. L'Maître was a Dominican friar of the convent of Rouen. Appointed by Jean Graverent, the inquisitor of France, he should have been the chief of the two judges required in a properly conducted church inquisitorial trial. (All church trials were not part of the Inquisition, but Joan's was.) But he was reluctant to be there; "as much for the serenity of his conscience as for a more certain conduct of the trial, he did not wish to be involved in this present affair."[8] He argued that Cauchon was out of his jurisdiction (having "borrowed" the diocese of Rouen because Beauvais was then under French control), but for that very reason, Cauchon insisted on L'Maître's presence.

The trial began with several irregularities besides L'Maître's absence: any preliminary information prejudicial to Joan's religious conformity came from anonymous sources, and no formal charges had yet been brought against her.

"I SHOULD ANSWER YOU BRAVELY"

On Ash Wednesday, February 21, Joan is presented to the court and the trial officially opens. According to the transcript, she faced some forty-five intimidating persons: nine doctors of theology, four doctors of canon law, one doctor of both civil and canon law who held a J.U.D. (Juris Ultriusque Doctor) from Bologna, seven bachelors of theology, eleven licentiates in canon law and four in civil law, among others. She stood alone, without a lawyer to advise her, again contrary to the traditional procedures of the Inquisition.

At first Joan resisted swearing an oath, fearing that she would be asked to reveal the revelations given her by God "because I know from my visions that I must keep them secret."[9] She said she could tell the court only about "my father and mother, and everything that I have done since I took the road to come to France."[10] After hours of questioning and clarification, Joan was on her knees with her two hands on the missal, swearing to tell the truth about whatever would be asked her about her religious beliefs. The taking of an oath would continue to be a problem for her each of the times she was questioned, and she added, "But I shall never say everything that I know."[11]

Following the normal forms, she stated her name, the names of her father and mother, where she was born, her godfathers, godmothers and the priest who baptized her, and her age, "as best as I can tell, around nineteen years."[12] She refused to say the Pater Noster (the Our Father), unless Bishop Cauchon heard it from her in confession, a move which invoked him in his priestly role. She then complained about the "five Englishmen of the lowest rank" who were guarding her in prison.

On subsequent days she was asked about fighting at Saint-Denis, before the city of Paris, on the feast day of the nativity of Mary. She insisted, "I have greater fear of failing my voices in saying something that displeases them than I have of answering you,"[13] and she responded to the devious question of whether her voices told her she would escape from prison, with "Do I have to tell you that?"[14] She never wavered about the supernatural character of her mission, referring frequently to her "voice" or "voices." This was a dangerous contention, claiming to be in communication with the world beyond.

"Do you know if you are in the grace of God?" asked one interrogator. "If I am not, may God put me there. And if I am, may God keep me there, for I would be the most sorrowful woman in the world if I knew that I was not in the grace of God."[15] Her eloquence "stupefied" her interrogators, notary Guillaume Bouille (also known as Guillaume Colles or Colles de Boisguillaume) recalled later at the nullification trial.[16] At this point, the record moves into indirect discourse, probably at Cauchon's order, in order to blunt the force of Joan's comments. From now on, it contains statements like, "She said that if she had been in sin, she thinks the voice would not have come to her, and she wished that everyone could hear it as well as herself."[17]

They questioned her a great deal about whether she had received her mission at the "Fairy Tree" in Domrémy, which would have indicated witchcraft. While she admitted singing around it with other children on village feasts, she denied a major connection with the tree. She also put off any charges of sorcery by answering about the pennons used by the French army and the child whom she supposedly restored back to life long enough to be baptized at Lagny. She expressed her faith when questioned about her leap from the tower at Beaurevoir: "I would prefer to surrender my soul to God than to be in the hands of the English."[18]

On February 27, Joan revealed the names of her voices: Saint Catherine, Saint Margaret and Saint Michael, who came first. She explained that the voice she heard last Saturday "told me that I should answer you bravely."[19] Then the question of her wearing men's clothes is brought up, to which she answers: "The clothes are a small matter, the least of all things; and I did not take up men's clothes on the advice of this world. I neither put on these clothes nor did I do anything except by the commandment of God and his angels."[20] On several different occasions, this question of male attire is brought up.

The interrogators tried to trick her into disclosing her revelations regarding the king of France, "the king's sign," crown and eventual victory, and such burning questions of the church at the time as the true pope and whether her saints had hair or wore clothes and what language they spoke. In the end, Joan replied that she doesn't care about such things; she only knows "I have great joy when I see him [Saint Michael]."[21]

Joan told the court that her voices had promised that she would be "delivered" through this trial ordeal, "but I do not know the day or the hour, and they said that I should bravely maintain a good face."[22] Whether Joan was thinking of spiritual deliverance or deliverance by death or physical rescue is not known.

At various points during the trial, Joan complains that she could not hear her voices. The presence of the English guards outside and inside her jail cell, with their loud and constant talking, insults and swearing, may be drowning out the divine communication she knew throughout most of her life. Her tension and fear don't help either. Her mood goes up and down, as well. The absence of her voices scares her more than the trial. Has God abandoned her?

DEFYING THE CHURCH MILITANT

After eleven days of public interrogation, the trial moved to Joan's jail cell. On March 10 Bishop Cauchon entered her cell, accompanied by three others, including Jean de la Fontaine. This lawyer began by asking Joan about the circumstances of her capture and the warnings her voices had given her at that point, but also took the time to caution her that, "if she did not declare her submission to the pope and to the Council, she would put herself 'in great danger.'"[23] For this sympathetic gesture toward Joan and later for taking the time to explain to Joan what the "Church Militant" is (the Catholic church on earth, as opposed to the Church Triumphant in heaven or the Church Suffering in purgatory), he incurred Cauchon's displeasure. After March 28, 1430, de la Fontaine took no further part in the trial and left Rouen (some say he was forced out by Cauchon).

Joan was totally alone. Constant surveillance and trickery insured that she had no counsel from the outside and that any of her words could be used against her. Her guards were charged with reporting to Cauchon anything they overheard from her cell. Joan was surprised to discover that among those present in court was the priest Nicolas Loiseleur, who had claimed to hail from the banks of the Meuse as she did, and be a fellow prisoner. He offered to hear her confession, and did. A notary had been ordered to hide in a nook that opened onto Joan's cell to in order to overhear what "she was saying or confessing to the aforesaid Loiseleur."[24]

This question of submission to the Church Militant was raised some twenty times after de la Fontaine mentioned it. Joan's answer, which took her some time to formulate, should have resolved the problem: "It is my sense that it is all one [Militant, Triumphant and Suffering], God's and the church's, and that there should be no difficulty about it. Why do you make difficulties about its being one and the same thing?"[25] Her impatience with what she considered theological subtleties was growing. For her, the faith was very simple. But the assessors continued to press the point, and in the end it became one of the formal accusations that could be brought against her.

Seventy articles were read out to Joan on March 27 and 28, from carrying a mandrake for luck and practicing divination (both of which she denied) to the wearing of male attire and refusal to submit to the Church Militant.

The assessors tried to blackmail her into wearing women's clothes, promising her that if she did, she would be able to attend Easter Mass. Even though Joan proposed some compromises, she apparently was denied the comfort of Easter Mass and Communion (in those days, most people received the Eucharist only on Easter).

Her response to submitting to the Church Militant is eloquent:

So long as she [the church] does not command something impossible to do—and what I call impossible is that I revoke the deeds I have done and the words I have said in this trial concerning the visions and revelations that were given to me from God, for I will not revoke them for anything; what Our Lord has made me do and has commanded and may yet command, I shall not fail to do for the sake of any man alive, and should the church wish that I do something against the commandment that was given me by God, I would not do it for anything.

When her questioner asked, "If the Church Militant tells you that your revelations are illusions or somehow diabolic, would you defer to the church?" she responded, "In that case, I would defer as always to God, whose command I have always obeyed.... It would be impossible for me to do the contrary."[26]

The week after Easter the seventy articles against her were reduced to twelve.

DID THE BISHOP POISON HER?

On April 18, Joan was ill and vomiting, which she attributed to eating a carp. Jean d'Estivet, canon of the Beauvais and Bayeux cathedrals, brought a doctor, Jean Tiphaine, the duchess of Bedford's own physician, to Joan's cell to check her out. When Joan said that the carp had been sent to her by Bishop Cauchon, the doctor recalled at her nullification trial that "Estivet reproached her, saying that what she had said was false; he called her a slut, saying: 'It's you, slut, who ate a shad and other things that have made you sick';...they exchanged lots of insulting words."[27]

It's easy for fish to go bad, so this incident may have been a pure accident. But the timing raises the question of whether Cauchon, frustrated in his attempt to lock up the case against her, had chosen to go the route of deliberately poisoning her. The extreme reaction of his close supporter Estivet supports that interpretation.

Pope Martin V had died on February 20, and his successor, Eugenius IV, had opposed many of the assessors at Joan's trial, so Cauchon, who had just learned this, was worried that support for Joan's trial would evaporate. The charges against Joan were now down to two, a thin basis for condemnation. But Cauchon's English friends had made it clear to him that they wanted Joan "formally condemned in a way that would entail both dishonor and discredit for Charles VII."[28] Time was running out for Cauchon.

That April 18 meeting was to have been devoted to what was called a "charitable warning," as Inquisition procedures proscribe, but Joan felt so poorly she thought she was in danger of death. She told the bishop, "I hope that the church and Catholic people will pray for me."[29] By May 2, the time of Joan's second "charitable warning," she had regained her strength and resolution, stating: "I believe fully in the church here below. I believe that the Church Militant cannot err or fail; but as far as what I have said and what I have done, I rely entirely on God, who has made me do what I have done."[30] She even offered to answer directly to the pope for what she had done.

On May 10, in the great tower of the castle (rather than the hall of judgment), Cauchon and some of the assessors threatened her with torture, to which she responded: "Truly, if you pull my members apart and make the soul leave the body, I will not tell you anything else, and if I should tell you something, afterward I shall always say that you made me say it by force."[31] Cauchon decided to postpone the decision on torturing Joan until he was sure of more support from his colleagues, but only three of the dozen assessors assembled that day judged it "expedient" to torture her to "know the truth about her lies."[32]

JOAN'S "CONFESSION"

On the Thursday after Pentecost, May 24, Cauchon masterminded a spectacle for Joan at the nearby cemetery of the Abbey of Saint-Ouen, where he had her brought. He had platforms set up for Joan and various dignitaries, including bishops and abbots. He had Guillame Érard, canon of Rouen and a master of the University of Paris, preach a fiery sermon against her, referring to her as "a

monster" and "this woman, this magician, heretical and supersti-
tious."[33] Joan repeatedly delivered her refrain: "As to my words and
deeds, I have done them on God's orders and charge no one else
with them, neither my king nor any other."[34] She again appealed to
be allowed to present her case to the pope in Rome.

But this request was denied. Instead, she was presented with a
cedula, a piece of parchment designed to be attached to a legal document. What was on that parchment? It was a letter of abjuration,
which would cancel out everything Joan had said at her trial. It
included a promise that she would no longer wear men's clothes.
Joan's request to have explained to her what she was signing was
turned down. Jean Massieu, who served as an usher-lawyer during
the condemnation trial, urged her to sign it but said later, "I saw
clearly that she did not understand this document."[35] Canon Érard
told her, if she didn't sign it, "you will end your days by fire."[36]

Joan appended her signature, adding a cross to her mark. Then,
according to the notary Guillaume Manchon, she laughed. The use
of the cross may have been part of the military code the French had
been using which indicated that what preceded it should be disre-
garded. According to eyewitnesses, what she signed was six or eight
lines long. In the trial transcript, the letter of abjuration runs forty-
seven lines in French (fifty-four in Latin).

"JUDICIAL MURDER"

For the next three days Joan wore a woman's dress, but then as
explained in Day Three of this retreat, she "relapsed" into wearing
men's clothes. "Only those who had relapsed—that is, those who
having once abjured their errors returned to them—could be condemned to death by a tribunal of the Inquisition and delivered for
death 'to the secular arm.'"[37]

On Sunday, May 27, Cauchon heard that she had returned to wearing men's clothes and went with the vice-inquisitor and several others to the prison to verify this. He asked her why she had done this and she replied that it was "more lawful and convenient... because I am with men."[38] She explained that she had signed the cedula only out of "fear of the fire"[39] and that God, through Saint Catherine and Saint Margaret, had told her he had "great sorrow" that she had consented in adjuring, that her signing and abjuration was "treason" and "I was damning myself to save my life."[40]

On May 29 Cauchon convened forty-two assessors to ask what should be done. Thirty-nine of them wanted her letter of abjuration read to her again, but Cauchon as chief judge (and the only remaining judge, as vice-inquisitor L'Maitre is conveniently absent) overruled them. Technically, the assessors are only advisory, so in the absence of L'Maitre, Cauchon's authority is absolute. In his haste, Cauchon committed yet another legal error. He didn't bother to secure a secular court's sentence of death. Cauchon later said to several Englishmen, including Warwick, who had waited in the open court of the castle, "Farewell, make good cheer. It is done."[41]

Early on May 30, Dominicans Martin Ladvenu and his assistant, Jean Toutmouillé, went to Joan's cell to bring her some spiritual comfort. Ladvenu heard her confession and told her that she had been sentenced to die that day. Her reaction to the news was "to cry out sorrowfully and pitiably to tear and pull her hair. 'Alas! that they treat me so horribly and cruelly that my body, clean and whole, which was never corrupted, should be today consumed and reduced to ashes!... Ah, I protest before God, the Great Judge, the great wrongs and grievances that they have done me.'"[42]

The usher Massieu heard from Ladvenu that Joan wished to receive the Eucharist, but he didn't know whether he should give Communion to an excommunicate. Surprisingly, Ladvenu received permission from Bishop Cauchon to do so: "Let them give her the sacrament of the Eucharist and anything she asks."[43] Massieu went to find a stole and candle, so that the sacrament could have as much dignity as possible. Nothing more than this act of charity actually reveals Cauchon's duplicity and knowledge that this was foremost a political trial. For Robert Wirth, Cauchon's allowing Joan to receive Communion shows that he knew he was participating in "judicial murder."[44] The mysteries shrouding the slow end of Joan's life," comments Siobhan Nash-Marshall,

> all point to a sinister plot behind Joan's death. Someone wanted her to suffer a painful public death, and that someone wanted to make sure that the death was perceived as an act of God's—or one which was in accord with his will. This explains the discrepancies between the public and private treatment of Joan on the day that she died.[45]

WHEN POLITICS MASQUERADES AS FAITH

It is hard to put ourselves back in Joan's world where time is measured according to the church's feasts and where we don't know the issues and alliances at stake. So what can we learn from Joan's trial?

First, it speaks of the danger inherent in confusing political motives with religious ones. Cauchon clearly is acting more out of his politics than his faith. Whenever the two are confused, it is the respect for the church that suffers. Recent examples, from liberation theology to the Christian Coalition, only confirm this.

Second, the church, which has the constant guidance of the Holy Spirit, still can be wrong on occasion. It is in the hands of men (and women) who don't always listen to the Spirit or their better instincts. This was acknowledged publicly by Pope John Paul II on Ash Wednesday, 2000, as part of the Great Millennium's Day of Atonement. In St. Peter's Square, the pope (assisted by Cardinal Joseph Ratzinger, who has since become Pope Benedict XVI) asked for pardon for sins that the church has committed in the service of truth, like the Crusades. No doubt, his apology also covers the sentencing of Joan of Arc.

Third, it was Joan's perseverance through her imprisonment, long trial, incessant questioning and her insistence on following God's commands, which made her a saint, not her military endeavors.

Fourth, the simple often can confound the wise because they can see to the heart of things. Or as Antoine de Saint Exupéry had the fox tell the Little Prince, "It is only with the heart that one can see rightly; what is essential is invisible to the eye."[46] Joan cuts to the heart of theological questions.

Fifth, it is important that we "speak truth to power," especially on behalf of the poor, the vulnerable, children and the aged, those who cannot speak for themselves.

Sixth, we should support those organizations that agitate on behalf of prisoners, like the efforts of the Innocence Project of Wisconsin and Northwestern University's Law School to free the unjustly accused. The police themselves admit that they sometimes have tunnel vision in centering in on someone for a crime too fast. Now that DNA evidence can be used, suspects' innocence can be given a fairer hearing and those falsely imprisoned exonerated.

In the end, Cauchon's apparent victory over Joan actually helped the French cause. In prosecuting her so vigorously (and largely illegally), he opened the door for declaring her trial null twenty-six years later.

For Reflection

1. Where do you find your villainous Cauchons? If you were put on trial, what might people say for and against you?

2. When it seems that they are opposed, would you defer to the church or to God?

3. Do you think Joan knew what she was signing with the cedula? What do you think she meant with her signature?

4. What do you think the pope would have done had he been alerted to Joan's situation?

5. Should Bishop Cauchon have allowed Joan Communion at the end? What do his actions say about the nature of the charges brought against Joan?

Closing Prayer

Dear God,

give me:

Joan's courage when I am under verbal assault,

words as eloquent as hers when I am overwhelmed by injustice,

tolerance of those who cannot see my point of view,

patience with the repetitiveness in life,

even with the simple tasks like laundry and fixing dinner for my family,

making one more sale or answering one more student's question.

Let me come to terms with the imperfections of our church, insofar as they reflect our own imperfections.

Teach me to forgive those who speak and work against me, letting me remember that you alone are the Great Judge, who knows all about the wrongs and grievances done me and that I do.

Forgive me when I forget your commands and
refuse to forgive in your name.

Amen.

Notes

1. Mary Gordon, *Joan of Arc* (New York: Penguin, 2000), p. 109.
2. Pernoud and Clin, p. 104.
3. Pernoud and Clin, p. 210.
4. Pernoud and Clin, pp. 123–124.
5. Pernoud and Clin, p. 107.
6. Pernoud and Clin, p. 104.
7. Pernoud and Clin, p. 105.
8. Pernoud and Clin, p. 108.
9. Pernoud and Clin, p. 109.
10. Pernoud and Clin, p. 109.
11. Pernoud and Clin, p. 111.

12. Pernoud and Clin, p. 109.
13. Pernoud and Clin, p. 111.
14. Pernoud and Clin, p. 111.
15. Pernoud and Clin, pp. 111–112.
16. T. Douglas Murray's notes of the file (London: William Heinemann Publisher, 1903), www.jeanne-darc.dk.
17. Pernoud and Clin, p. 112.
18. Pernoud and Clin, p. 117.
19. Pernoud and Clin, p. 113.
20. Pernoud and Clin, p. 114.
21. Pernoud and Clin, p. 116.
22. Pernoud and Clin, p. 116.
23. Pernoud and Clin, p. 117.
24. Pernoud and Clin, p. 111.
25. Pernoud and Clin, p. 122.
26. Pernoud and Clin, pp. 123–124.
27. Pernoud and Clin, p. 125.
28. Pernoud and Clin, p. 126.
29. Pernoud and Clin, p. 127.
30. Pernoud and Clin, p. 127.
31. Pernoud and Clin, p. 127.
32. Pernoud and Clin, p. 128.
33. Pernoud and Clin, p. 130.
34. Pernoud and Clin, p. 130.
35. Pernoud and Clin, p. 130.
36. Pernoud and Clin, p. 131.
37. Pernoud and Clin, p. 132.
38. Pernoud and Clin, p. 133.
39. *Joan of Arc: In Her Own Words*, Willard Trask, trans. (New York: Turtle Point, 1996), p. 139.
40. Pernoud and Clin, p. 133.
41. Pernoud and Clin, p. 133.
42. Pernoud and Clin, pp. 133–134.
43. Pernoud and Clin, p. 134.
44. Robert Wirth, www.joanofarc@seas.smu.edu, June 22, 1999, reported by Pernoud and Clin, p. 134.
45. Nash-Marshall, p. 22.
46. Antoine de Saint Exupéry, *The Little Prince*, Katherine Woods, trans. (New York: Harcourt, Brace & World, 1943), p. 87.

DAY SEVEN

FOCUSING

ON

THE CRUCIFIX

La Hire: We were fools to burn Joan of Arc.

Cauchon: We committed a sin, a monstrous sin.

Warwick: Yes, it was a grave mistake. We made a lark into a giant bird who will travel the skies of the world long after our names are forgotten, or confused, or cursed down.

La Hire: I knew the girl and I loved her. You can't let it end this way. If you do, it will not be the true story of Joan.

Ladvenu: That is right. The true story of Joan is not the hideous agony of a girl tied to a burning stake. She will stand forever for the glory that can be. Praise God.

—*The Lark*, Act Two[1]

COMING TOGETHER IN THE SPIRIT

Bishop Cauchon had ordered that Joan be burned immediately at the stake prepared in the Old Marketplace. (Today a sixty-five-foot-high *Croix de la Réhabilitation* [Rehabilitation Cross] stands on the very spot where Joan was burned on May 30, 1430. Next to it is a modern church built in the shape of an upturned ship, which was completed in 1979.)

Cauchon had several platforms set up on the market square, just as he had arranged in the Saint-Ouen cemetery. When Joan arrived by cart at the marketplace, she had to endure an oration from Nicolas Midi, a theologian who had just eleven days before been installed as a canon of Rouen cathedral. (When Midi contracted leprosy sometime around 1434, it was interpreted as a sign of divine punishment for his role in Joan's trial and execution.) Perhaps as many as eight hundred armed men (the regular castle garrison and those assembling for an attack on Louviers) witnessed her execution.

But Joan's death did not stop her legend. Her death, as described by many eyewitnesses, is a perfect example of keeping faith to the end. It has inspired many martyrs since.

OPENING PRAYER

God,
Joan kept her eyes glued on the crucifix
when she burned at the stake.
In that crucifix she recognized all you had suffered for us,
and that sustained her to the end.
Then you gathered your faithful servant Joan to yourself
and left us with her example to follow.
Amen.

RETREAT SESSION SEVEN

"Hold the crucifix up before my eyes that I may see it until I die."
—Joan of Arc from her burning pyre to
Friar Isambert de la Pierre[2]

"Jesus! Jesus!"

—Joan's last words[3]

There seems to be some debate as to whether Joan died by burning or asphyxiation, whether the wood was green and what effect that might have had, but there is no doubt that she died there, in that marketplace in Rouen.

From the pyre, she asked for a cross. First, some Englishman roughly fashioned one for her. Joan kissed it and tucked it into her bosom. Then Friar de la Pierre went to the nearby church of Saint-Laurent for a cross "to hold elevated right above her eyes up to the moment of death, so that the cross on which God hung during His life could be continually before her sight."[4] A number of witnesses remarked that she continued to proclaim the name of Jesus, repeating it with her dying breath.

When she died, an Englishman who "detested her exceptionally and had sworn that with his own hand he would bring a bundle of sticks to Joan's stake,"[5] swore that, at the moment of her death, he had seen a white dove come out of her and take flight toward French-occupied territory. Several battle-scarred veterans observing her death wept openly. It was reported that the secretary to the king of England, Jean Tressart, was much affected by her death, lamenting, "We are all lost, for it is a good and holy person that was burned."[6] One of the assessors at Joan's trial, Jean Alespée, another canon of Rouen, was among those weeping at her death and supposedly said, "I wish that my soul were where I believe this woman's soul is."[7]

Warwick ordered her ashes to be collected and thrown into the Seine River, so that no relics of her could be claimed and taken into battle.

JOAN'S REPUTATION RESTORED

After the execution, Bishop Cauchon would brook no criticism. When a Dominican from the convent of Saint-Jacques (home to Friars Ladvenu and de la Pierre) suggested that those who had judged Joan had done wrong, Cauchon sentenced him to ten months in prison on bread and water. Cauchon continued trying to get the record of the trial rewritten and to compel the assessors to agree that Joan had formally denied her voices. Cauchon's death while being shaved in 1442 was considered divine retribution for unjustly sentencing Joan—by her supporters, at least. After all, she had warned him, "Be careful, you who call yourself my judge! Be careful about what you are doing, because my quest does come from God, and you are taking a terrible risk!"[8]

Joan's execution was the beginning of the end for the Hundred Years' War. After her death, the English and their supporters knew that they were fighting a losing battle for a hopeless cause. Joan had given hope and renewed energy to her people.

After a number of decisive military victories, King Charles VII decided to show his gratitude for Joan and what she had done to secure his throne. In 1449 he asked Pope Nicholas V to authorize a new trial for Joan. But it was the next pope, Calixtus III, who ordered it in 1455. Bishop Cauchon and several of the other protagonists had died by then. Twenty-seven articles addressed specific points of irregularity in the trial, like Joan not being allowed a lawyer. In Rouen on July 7, 1456, after a two-year legal process, the 1431 trial was officially nullified. A copy of the trial transcript was torn up in a formal ceremony in the episcopal palace in Rouen.

Pierre Duparc's 1988 Latin and French critical edition of the nullification trial's transcript contains not just the eyewitness testimony about Joan's life, but reflections of bishops, clerics and lawyers who raise such provocative and contemporary questions such as, "How can we judge a claim of mystical experience?" and "Can truth be discovered through torture and fear?"

Of course, the verdict of the nullification didn't do anything for Joan, but it did bring some comfort to her mother. And it legitimated the cult of Joan, which eventually resulted in her canonization in 1920.

SINGLE-MINDED FOR GOD

Why did Joan's sainthood take so long for the whole church to acknowledge? Probably because of the complex issues her life and death raise—and politics in the church and society.

Even though she died young—still a teenager—Joan's example of dying well can be an inspiration for all who are facing decline and death. She had received warnings of her death from her voices, which had somewhat prepared her to accept it.

Her piety seems quaint to us, just as it must have to the sophisticated and learned of her own time. But there's no doubt that her focus on Jesus and his sacrificial death on the cross for us should always be our focus, too. All the great saints have been single-minded for God. That's our calling as well.

FOR REFLECTION

1. If you had been at Joan's execution, what do you suppose you would have seen and thought?
2. Do you think Bishop Cauchon tolerated no criticism because he knew he was guilty of sentencing an innocent woman? Do you think others responsible for Joan's death ever realized what they had done?
3. What difference did Joan's nullification trial make?
4. Do you know someone who's been maligned and whose reputation you could help restore?
5. Was Joan too simplistic in her theology?
6. Why did Joan's canonization take so long? What does her canonization mean to us?

Closing Prayer

Dear God,

Joan focused her entire life on you,

even in the pain of her fiery death.

Help me to keep a single-minded focus on you,

in all that I do,

despite all distractions and temptations,

like power, money, ego.

Joan stayed true to you to the end;

help me to follow her example.

Adjust my compass so that I am always coming closer to you,

always honing in on you.

When my time comes,

help me to die bravely and

throw myself into your loving arms.

I know that you will be there for me

because you always have been there for me.

I'll just be coming home

where I hope to meet this intriguing saint.

Amen.

Notes

1. Jean Anouilh, *The Lark*, adapted by Lillian Hellman (New York: Random House, 1955, 1956), pp. 142–143.
2. http://www.stjoan-center.com/quotable.
3. http://www.stjoan-center.com/quotable.
4. Pernoud and Clin, p. 136.
5. Pernoud and Clin, p. 136.
6. Pernoud and Clin, p. 137.
7. Pernoud and Clin, p. 137.
8. Nash-Marshall, p. 13.

GOING FORTH TO LIVE THE THEME

J OAN OF ARC IS LIKE A SHOOTING STAR ACROSS THE LANDSCAPE OF
French and English history, amid the stories of the church's saints
and into our consciousness. Women identify with her; men admire
her courage. She challenges us in fundamental ways. Despite the
fact that more than five hundred years have passed since she lived,
her issues of mysticism, calling, identity, trust and betrayal, conflict
and focus are our issues still.

Joan began with peculiar, intimate communication from and
with God and was moved to work for justice on earth, as theologian
George H. Tavard points out. "Her life offers a perfect example of the
conjunction of contemplation and action," because her spiritual
insight is that there should be a "unity of heaven and earth."[1]

Joan persevered in her faith, accepting her many crosses for the
sake of the Cross. She remained steadfast in her mission, having ful-
filled Saint Paul's admonition to "Fight the good fight of the faith" (1
Timothy 6:12). In fact, she has much in common with Saint Paul,
who admits to "visions and revelations" (2 Corinthians 12:1) and
"talking like a madman" (2 Corinthians 11:23); started his ministry
"in weakness and in fear and in much trembling" (1 Corinthians
2:3); is boastful, especially in God's promises and strength; advises
us to "become fools so that you may become wise" (1 Corinthians

3:18); and in the end rejoices that "I have fought the good fight, I have finished the race, I have kept the faith" (2 Timothy 4:7).

Here I have chosen to stick very closely to what can be historically proven about Joan, relying primarily on Régine Pernoud and Marie-Véronique Clin's well-documented *Joan of Arc: Her Story*. Lots of her biographers and commentators include other information, some from their own imaginations, and offer more speculation than I have here—all to support their take on her. I'm sorry if I have not included your favorite Joan story or movie interpretation, but she's one of the most written-about saints. Supplement my retelling and commentary with whatever inspires you.

James Martin, s.j., associate editor of *America,* attributes his lifelong fascination with Joan to the "marvelous illogic of her story."[2] She was the first saint he really "met," he says. "And like my introduction to French in high school, Joan's story also introduced me to a new language: the special language of saints, made up of verbs like to *believe, pray, witness* and the nouns of their actions, *humility, charity, ardor.*"[3]

Martin continues:

> Yet Joan confuses me as much as she attracts me. She acts like a crazy young girl, hearing voices, leaving her family, going to war, and dying for an unseen person. Her story is more profoundly *other* than those of almost any other saint…. Even St. Francis of Assisi would seem more at home in our world than Joan.[4]

Joan helped him to discover his vocation as a Jesuit, Martin admits. "Joan found her way to God by learning a language that no one else could hear, and so is the perfect model for someone on the beginning of a faith journey. She had no idea what path to take to reach her destination, and neither did I."[5]

One of Joan of Arc's "daughters," Joan Chittister, O.S.B., a social activist and well-known author, includes the following prayer to Joan among the twenty-two litanies of saints and holy people in her new book, *Prayer for Conscience and Courage in Times of Public Struggle*:

> St. Joan of Arc,
> you were burned at the stake
> as a heretic by the church itself
> for refusing to betray
> the voice of God in you.
> Touch our conscience
> on behalf of the visionaries
> in church and society
> and give us the courage
> to share the risk.[6]

I hope that through these pages you have met a fascinating woman who has challenged you to grow in your faith. I know that Joan, my own patron saint, continues to inspire me.

Notes
1. Tavard, pp. 170, 169.
2. James Martin, S.J., *My Life With the Saints* (Chicago: Loyola, 2006), p. 22.
3. Martin, p. 25.
4. Martin, p. 25.
5. Martin, p. 26.
6. Joan Chittister, *Prayer for Conscience and Courage in Time of Public Struggle* (Erie, Pa.: Benetvision, 2007).

DEEPENING YOUR ACQUAINTANCE

THE FOLLOWING BOOKS, VIDEOS, DVDS AND CDS, AS well as Web sites, are intended to help retreatants sustain their relationship with Joan of Arc. Because of the wealth of material available about her life and its significance for us, I have chosen to annotate this bibliography.

Books

Anouilh, Jean. *The Lark,* adapted by Lillian Hellman (New York: Dramatists Play Service, 1998). This was the New York production of the 1955 play *L'Alouette,* which starred Julie Christie and Boris Karloff. Anouilh's play is a Frenchman's take on Joan as a classic heroine of resistance.

Brooks, Polly Schoyer. *Beyond the Myth: The Story of Joan of Arc* (Boston: Houghton Mifflin, 1990). *School Library Journal* called this, "The definitive Joan of Arc biography for young adults." It's quite readable for "old adults," too, as it supplies motivation and background information on Joan's world. A teacher, Brooks also wrote a biography about Eleanor of Acquitaine: *Queen Eleanor: Independent Spirit of the Medieval World* (Houghton Mifflin) and developed curricula for the New Canaan, Connecticut, school system.

De Wohl, Louis. *Saint Joan: The Girl Soldier* (San Francisco: Ignatius, 2001; originally published by Farrar, Straus and Cudahy, 1957). Illustrated by Harry Barton. Writing for young adults, de Wohl emphasizes Joan's all-encompassing love of God and says, "...[S]aints make history, and what is more, they make it the way God likes it best."

Gordon, Mary. *Joan of Arc* (New York: Viking, 2000). An elegantly written biography, this well-known novelist deals with the mysteries in the life of this "least likely of heroines."

Nash-Marshall, Siobhan. *Joan of Arc: A Spiritual Biography.* Lives and Legacies series, edited by Barbara Leah Ellis (New York: Crossroad, 1999). This book explores "the terror she caused, the love she inspired and the nation she created."

Pernoud, Régine, and Marie-Véronique Clin. *Joan of Arc: Her Story,* translated and revised by Jeremy duQuesnay Adams, edited by Bonnie Wheeler (New York: Palgrave Macmillan, 1999). Originally published as *Jeanne d'Arc,* Régine Pernoud and M.-V. Clin (Paris: Librarie Arthème Fayard, 1986). Pernoud was "the grande dame of French historical writing on the Middle Ages" and founder of the Centre Jeanne d'Arc in Orléans; Clin is director of the Museum of the History of Medicine in Paris and of the Centre Jeanne d'Arc in Paris; duQuesnay Adams is a professor of history at Southern Methodist University; Wheeler is his wife, director of medieval studies at SMU and director of the International Joan of Arc Society. This is a different kind of biography because it doesn't start when Joan was born but when she first appears in the historical record (just before the battle for Orleans). Half of the book is excellent collateral material: black-and-white representations of Joan, further information on the "cast of characters" and issues in her drama, her letters, chronology and itinerary, maps, bibliography and a thorough index. Simply the best!

Pernoud, Régine. *Those Terrible Middle Ages: Debunking the Myths,* translated by Anne Englund Nash (San Francisco: Ignatius, 2000). This gives a wonderful background on Joan's times.

Richey, Stephen W. *Joan of Arc: The Warrior Saint* (Westport, Conn.: Praeger, 2003). This is primarily an analysis of Joan's military skills by a professional soldier.

Shaw, Bernard. *Saint Joan: A Chronicle Play in Six Scenes and an Epilogue* (London: Penguin, 2001). This is the definitive text under the editorial supervision of Dan H. Laurence, and includes the essay "On Playing Joan," by Imogen Stubbs, and an introduction by Joley Wood, which predicts, "[W]ere Joan alive today, she would still be persecuted." The play was first produced in New York in 1923 and in London in 1924, and first published by Penguin Books in 1946.

Spoto, Donald. *Joan: The Mysterious Life of the Heretic Who Became a Saint* (San Francisco: HarperSanFrancisco, 2007). Fresh from his successful biography and movie about Saint Francis of Assisi, Spoto tackles another difficult saint. Concluding that Joan "demonstrates that anyone who follows their heart has the power to change history," the book is readable, balanced and meticulously researched.

Tavard, George H. *The Spiritual Way of St. Jeanne d'Arc* (Collegeville, Minn.: Liturgical, 1998). This book from an Augustinian priest, who was born in the same area as Joan and as a youth visited the places important in her life; it looks at her spirituality particularly as articulated in the responses she gave at her trial in Rouen and through the witnesses at her rehabilitation trial.

Trask, Willard R. *Joan of Arc: In Her Own Words,* (New York: Turtle Point, 1996). Scholar and translator Trask draws Joan's words mostly from her testimony at her trial and orders them according to the events in her life. He does, however, take the liberty of restoring some passages of indirect discourse into first person.

Twain, Mark. *Joan of Arc* (San Francisco: Ignatius, 1989). This work was first serialized in *Harper's* magazine and ostensibly presented as a recent translation by Jean François Alden of the memoir of Sieur Louis de Conte, Joan's page and secretary, who knew her as a villager, military genius and defendant at trial. Because of that conceit, it's difficult to get into. But Twain's love of Joan comes through and carries it off.

Wallace, Susan Helen, F.S.P., *Saint Joan of Arc: God's Soldier* (Boston, Mass.: Pauline Books and Media, 2000), illustrated by Ray Morelli. This is part of Pauline's Encounter the Saints series for young people.

Wheeler, Bonnie, and Charles T. Wood, editors, *Fresh Verdicts on Joan of Arc* (New York: Garland, 1996). These scholarly, interdisciplinary essays cover such diverse topics as the lost record of Joan's interrogation at Poitiers, identification of Joan's voices, cross-dressing, Joan in the cinema, the "Joan Phenomenon" and material aspects of the culture of her time.

VIDEOS, DVDs AND CDs

Joan of Arc, with Leelee Sobieski, Jacqueline Bisset, Neil Patrick Harris, Robert Loggia, Peter Strauss, Peter O'Toole, Maximilian Schell, Olympia Dukakis and Shirley MacLaine, directed by Christian Duguay. (Alliance Atlantis/Artisan Home Entertainment, 1999). 180 minutes.

"Joan of Arc: Virgin Warrior," part of the Arts and Entertainment Channel's Legendary Women series on *Biography* (A&E Television Network, 1998). 50 minutes.

Joan of Arc: Child of War, Soldier of God, narrated by Alfred Molina, with the voice of Anna Paquin as Joan and Lucie Vondráčková as Joan. (Faith and Values Media, distributed by Lightworks, 2005). 60 minutes.

The Messenger: The Story of Joan of Arc, with Milla Jovovich, John Malkovich, Faye Dunaway and Dustin Hoffman, directed by Luc Besson. (Columbia Pictures/Columbia Tristar Home Video, 2000). 158 minutes.

The Passion of Joan of Arc, with Renée Falconetti, directed by Carl Dreyer. (Home Vision Cinema, 1999). 82 minutes. This black-and-white, silent film from 1928 is presented with French intertitles and English subtitles. Considered "the greatest and most important silent film ever made," *The Passion of Joan of Arc* inspired Richard Einhorn's 1988 oratorio "Voices of Light," featuring soprano Susan Narucki and the Netherlands Radio Choir and the Netherlands Radio Philharmonic, which is packaged with it as a CD.

WEB SITES

On www.smu.edu/ijas the International Joan of Arc Society (Société Internationale de l'étude de Jeanne d'Arc) shares scholarly and pedagogic information about Joan of Arc, collected by faculty, independent scholars and students. Its director is Bonnie Wheeler.

On www.stjoan-center.com the Saint Joan of Arc Center maintains over one thousand pages that spread information and devotion to Saint Joan of Arc. Its address is: The Saint Joan of Arc Center, P. O. Box 13226, Albuquerque, NM 87912. The center's director is Virginia Frohlich.